the one percent *Miracle*

MARCIA HANSEN
LEXI HANSEN

the one percent *Miracle*

The Remarkable Story
of Modern-Day Miracles
and How Lexi Hansen
Beat the Odds

PLAIN SIGHT
PUBLISHING

AN IMPRINT OF CEDAR FORT, INC.
SPRINGVILLE, UTAH

ISBN 13: 978-1-4621-2180-9

Published by Plain Sight Publishing, an imprint of Cedar Fort, Inc.
2373 W. 700 S., Springville, UT 84663
Distributed by Cedar Fort, Inc., www.cedarfort.com

LIBRARY OF CONGRESS CATALOGING-IN-PUBLICATION DATA

Names: Hansen, Marcia, 1959- author. | Hansen, Lexi, 1995- author.
Title: The one percent miracle : the remarkable story of modern-day miracles
    and how Lexi Hansen beat the odds / Marcia Hansen and Lexi Hansen.
Description: Springville, Utah : Plain Sight Publishing, An imprint of Cedar
    Fort, Inc., [2018]
Identifiers: LCCN 2017038605 (print) | LCCN 2017042435 (ebook) | ISBN
    9781462128747 (epub and Moby) | ISBN 9781462121809 ([perfect] : alk. paper)
Subjects: LCSH: Hansen, Lexi, 1995- | Traffic accident victims--Biography. |
    Mormon youth--Biography. | LCGFT: Biographies.
Classification: LCC BX8695.H333 (ebook) | LCC BX8695.H333 H36 2018 (print) |
    DDC 289.3092 [B] --dc23
LC record available at https://lccn.loc.gov/2017038605

Cover design by Shawnda T. Craig
Cover design © 2018 by Cedar Fort, Inc.
Edited by Kyli Wright and Erica Myers
Typeset by Kaitlin Barwick

Printed in the United States of America

10 9 8 7 6 5 4 3 2 1

Printed on acid-free paper

*To Lexi Hansen and
all those who prayed for her*

CONTENTS

FOREWORD
BY TRAVIS J. NORTH

I am an emergency room social worker, also known as a crisis therapist. I often describe my job as helping people through what can generally be described as that person's worst day. Having worked in this position for a number of years, I can tell you it is not the same as is portrayed in television dramas. Not everyone survives, and there are a number of dark days. In my first shift on the job, three people passed away and another individual lost the ability to walk. I've personally experienced many days where I've felt devastated by the events I witnessed. I've genuinely pondered whether I could continue to be a part of the chaos. The senseless loss of promising lives forced me to question my belief in everything God has to offer.

I rarely talk about the devastation I see in the emergency room simply because it's difficult for people to hear. Many cannot extrapolate the lessons to be learned, or they lack the context to appreciate life's tragic events. Those that do often ask me, "Why do you stay? How can you continue working through such tragic circumstances?" My response can be summed up in one word: *Miracles*.

Although we'd all like to think we've lived a life worthy of experiencing a miracle, the sad truth is that miracles like Lexi's rarely happen, and certainly not just because we desire it. I don't know why I've been so blessed to experience the many miracles I have. I have mourned with and comforted people in their darkest moments. I have observed people bargain, plead, and pray with every fiber of their soul, only to be let down and lose what they value most.

This story, Lexi's story, not only changed her life and the lives of her family, but it touched the lives of everyone who had the opportunity to work with her family in the hospital and the community at large who followed her story. Her story has the ability to change your life. I cannot explain why God spares some and lets others go, but I know that He desires us to learn, grow, and increase our faith through these stories and experiences. He also allows stories like Lexi's to serve as a reminder of who He is, of His ability to heal us both physically and emotionally, and of the love He has for all of his children.

—Travis J. North, BS, MSW, LCSW

ACKNOWLEDGMENTS

My family and I want to thank each person who fasted and prayed on behalf of Lexi. We are grateful for the love you showed us and for your unwavering support and encouragement. It is impossible to fully express our gratitude for the gift you gave to us. You have influenced our lives by your goodness.

My greatest earthly support was given to me by my husband, Doug, and my nine children and their spouses: Shae, McKay and Makana, JD and McCall, Shelby and Brandon, Cassidy and Daniel, Kelsi, Tanner and Amanda, Lexi, and Parker. Their love and support mean everything to me. They are the best of the best. I am blessed to be called their mother.

In addition, I am grateful for my deceased parents, who taught me about the Savior. I know that without their help this miracle would not have happened. They were with us every step of the way.

We are also indebted to the doctors and nurses who gave Lexi the best care possible and who did all they could to save her life.

Most of all, we know that we owe everything to the Lord for His constant watchful care over our family and for saving Lexi.

The time spent writing this book has been a source of joy and love for me as I have revisited all the blessings the Lord poured out upon our family. As Mary did, I have "kept all these things, and pondered them in [my] heart" (Luke 2:19). I wasn't sure if I should write about a subject that is so personal and sacred to me and my family, but I felt urged on by the Spirit to write so that others might know to a greater extent that God is *still* a God of miracles. I believe one reason this miracle occurred is because God wants us to call upon Him more often and with much more fervency than we are presently doing.

I am grateful for the editing done by my daughter-in-law Mandy and for the suggestions of my daughter Kelsi. The bulk of the editing was done by Sarah Monson, who also provided valuable and insightful suggestions that helped to make Lexi come alive to the readers, for which my gratitude is boundless.

PREFACE

My husband, Doug, and I met when we were in our third year of college. Our apartments were across the street from one another, and after a year of courtship, we were married. It was just a short ten months later when our first child, Shae, arrived. Our life would never be the same again—in a wonderful but exacting way.

Shae was born with many complications. She was deaf, somewhat intellectually disabled, and had cerebral palsy. We were told by our doctor, who was a member of our church, that if we had more children, they would most likely have the same disabilities or greater ones. He suggested that before we had more children, both my husband and I should make it a matter of prayer. We both felt at peace and had full faith that our future children would not have any problems. We then went on to have eight more children who were all born in good health. We could see that from the very beginning of our marriage, we had been blessed by the power of God in our lives.

I had always wanted to have a family of five children while my husband was happy to have just two kids. I was able to talk my husband into having more children when I reminded him of his heavy work schedule and that I would be the one taking care of the children almost entirely. And I soon found that

I enjoyed being a mother so much that I didn't want to stop after the fifth child.

Eighteen months after Shae was born, my oldest son, McKay, joined our family. He was studious, friendly, and more serious than his younger brother JD, who was born eighteen months later. JD was playful and loved to tease but was very loving. He and McKay became Shae's guardians. No one would hurt her when they were around.

Three sweet but lively girls—Shelby, Cassidy, and Kelsi, who could have passed as triplets—followed in the lineup. They were best friends. I would hear them giggling and talking for hours after I put them to bed.

Lexi was born with the last set of three children. She was bold, athletic, daring, and courageous, probably due to the fact that she was sandwiched in between her older brother Tanner and her younger brother, Parker. They watched out for her, she tried to keep up with them, and vice versa.

More than anything else, all nine of my children love the Lord and strive to follow Jesus Christ in word and deed.

We were not wealthy, which made having a large family difficult if we wanted to take the kids to exotic places. Yet we found having fun didn't have to cost money. It wasn't unusual to see our entire clan going for bike rides or walks in the neighborhood.

On hot summer days, we trudged up trails, enjoying the height and grandeur of the mountains and the wild flowers that lined the path and carpeted the hillside. Eating our packed lunch in the shadow of these majestic hills while skipping rocks in the crystal stream soothed our souls. In autumn, the spectacular color display continued to draw us to the hills. The cool, crisp air welcomed the kids as they scurried along the path in search of vividly colored leaves, tucking them inside their bags to keep their treasures safe.

Even in winter, we found inexpensive ways to bond. As silent snowflakes fell, the kids would trudge through mounds of sparkling snow, pulling sleds to the top of the hill before sailing down, splattering snow on their faces. Even when very young, Lexi always insisted on pulling her sled up the slope to the peak herself, only to see it slide back down without her time after time. Hot cocoa and a glowing fire awaited our return. We found it didn't take money to love, make memories, or discover the enchanting mystique of nature.

During the year, the kids made homemade presents to exchange with each other on Christmas Eve. There was always more excitement for the gift they had painstakingly made than the one present they would get from Santa. And I found it fascinating that even when we finally saved up enough money to move into a larger home with more bedrooms, I would find the kids all sleeping in the same room the next morning. They were each other's best friends.

Lexi loved being the second youngest; she was never in need of a friend. She followed her siblings' examples and was good, kind, and pleasant toward everyone.

In Lexi's senior high school yearbook, parents were given the opportunity to write a tribute for their son or daughter, which would appear alongside their child's yearbook photo. These are the words I penned less than a year before Lexi's accident:

> Lex has a contagious smile, radiates joy, and is unafraid. She is faithful, honorable, confident, smart, motivated, and beautiful inside and out. She's a tennis ace pro and an accomplished musician on the piano and violin. You are amazing!

If I could add a few more qualities to describe Lexi, I would also say she is one of the hardest-working people I know. We taught her that if she wanted to go to college or serve an LDS mission, she would have to pay for it herself. From a young age, she started babysitting to earn money and then worked her way up mowing lawns and doing landscape jobs all before she was sixteen years old. Almost all of the money she earned she put in the bank. After turning sixteen, she started working two to three jobs even though she was on the tennis team, in orchestra, and taking AP classes.

Her reward for paying her own way through college gave her a greater abundance of the Spirit and a work ethic that prepared her for her mission and for life. Through her efforts, she earned enough money to pay for her room and tuition and still had enough money left over to pay for her entire mission.

Lexi has always had a desire to help and serve others. In high school, she thought a way to do this was to get involved in student government her senior year. Her brother told her stories of new friendships he had made and service projects he had helped with because of his participation in student government, and she wanted to have the same experiences.

Lexi was well liked, had lots of friends, and spent tedious hours on her campaign designing posters and creating a skit. But sadly, after all her effort, she didn't win. I convinced her to not give up and to run for a class officer. But yet again, when the tallies came in, she came up short. Losing twice isn't easy for anyone, and she took it hard. She came home in tears and inconsolable.

Knowing that there was much more to life than an election, I said in effect, "Lex, God knows you. He knows what is best for you. This is a time you need to have faith in Him and His plan for you. Not just faith in Him, but faith that He is guiding your life. You did all you could, but for some reason, you were not to win. It's easy to have faith when everything is going good, but is that really strong faith if at the first sign of any affliction in your life, you give up? Trust Him. He does have something great in store for you."

She stopped crying, and her face softened. Being popular had never meant a great deal to her, but she had told me often that she felt like this would have been a way that she could influence more people in a positive way. That's what saddened her: feeling she had failed to do more good. But she believed me and threw her tears to the wind.

Sure enough, God did have a plan for her. Two weeks later, she was called to be the president of a religious service organization. Maybe it wasn't as glamorous a position, but she was elated. Her face seemed to dance with happiness. If she had been elected as a student body officer, she never would have been given this opportunity. She was selected by the faculty out of hundreds of students. I believe she was chosen because of her unwavering trust in God.

Truly, Lexi is a spiritual giant with incredible faith a rock. She is also unafraid to share her love of God and has always made it a point to tell others about Him.

Another reason I think she was chosen to be president of this religious institution was because of her sincere and pure love and kindness she showed toward everyone. For instance, it made no difference to Lexi if someone was popular or shy. She was their friend and showed genuine love no matter what. Many felt the influence of her words and actions.

Besides Lexi's great love for people, she has a wonderful joy for life that is an inspiration to others. Her million-dollar smile and contagious laugh convey this ability as well as the beauty of her spirit. There is a special light that shines from her eyes that is visible to all those around her. It testifies of her deep love for the Savior, Jesus Christ, so it makes perfect sense that Lexi's favorite scripture is found in Exodus 4:10–12.

> And Moses said unto the Lord, O my Lord, I am not eloquent, neither heretofore, nor since thou hast spoken unto thy servant: but I am slow of speech, and of a slow tongue.
>
> And the Lord said unto him, Who hath made man's mouth? or who maketh the dumb, or deaf, or the seeing, or the blind? have not I the Lord?
>
> Now therefore go, and I will be with thy mouth, and teach thee what thou shalt say.

She is the epitome of goodness.

Chapter One

THE MIRACLE OF THE SPIRIT'S PROMPTINGS

I have called thee by thy name; thou art mine. When thou passest through the waters, I will be with thee; and through the rivers, they shall not overflow thee: when thou walkest through the fire, thou shalt not be burned; neither shall the flame kindle upon thee. For I am the Lord thy God, the Holy One of Israel, thy Saviour. . . . Since thou wast precious in my sight, thou hast been honourable, and I have loved thee. . . . Fear not: for I am with thee.

—Isaiah 43:1–5

I had read and pondered this stirring scripture from Isaiah just a month prior to the accident. But now these tender and moving words became much more than a beautiful script on a page; they became a personal message to me from God. They seemed to leap off the page and into my heart. God was speaking directly to me. He had not forgotten me and would stay by my side as I passed through this profound challenge. I need not fear.

1

The night of February 26, 2014, is one I wish I could erase from my memory. I was home alone that evening and had just sat down to get a quick bite to eat when Doug came rushing in the door.

"The hospital called," came his staggering announcement.

"The hospital? You startled me. I wasn't expecting you to be here," I said. His statement did not sink in.

"They called me when they couldn't get hold of you. We have to go to the hospital. *Now!* Lexi was hit by a car." There was a touch of fear in his voice.

His words jolted me from my thoughts, and I bounded from the table and away from my quiet surroundings. I grew suddenly anxious, and there was pleading in my voice: "How bad is she? What type of injury did she sustain? Where is she? Did she break her leg?" My questions tumbled out one after the other.

> *Hast thou not known? Hast thou not heard, that the everlasting God, the Lord, the Creator of the ends of the earth, fainteth not, neither is weary? There is no searching of his understanding. He giveth power to the faint; and to them that have no might he increaseth strength.*
>
> —Isaiah 40:28–29

Doug shook his head and sighed deeply. "I have no idea."

I ran to grab my shoes and coat as I tried to make sense of what he was saying. He seemed alarmed and concerned, but I couldn't accept what might really have happened. I thought he might be overreacting, and I wanted reassurance that indeed Lexi's injuries weren't major and that she would be fine. In my mind, they just couldn't possibly be considered fatal. Serious accidents happened to other people, but they couldn't possibly happen to me or my family! I was to discover soon enough that I was in for a rude awakening.

I continued my round of relentless questions as we flew out the door and jumped in the car. He responded in the same way no matter how I made my inquiries: "I don't know; it doesn't look good. We need to hurry," he repeated, trying to appease me. His demeanor told me it was much worse than what I had imagined. He continued, "The doctor just told me that we needed to get there as fast as we could."

It was dusk and the roads were congested from commuters leaving work, but that didn't deter my husband from speeding and weaving through the traffic to get to Lexi's side at Utah Valley Regional Medical Center, about forty minutes from our home.

Lexi was in her second semester of college. She was fiercely independent and had been excited to live in a dorm with roommates she had never met. She was passionate about learning and would only talk to me about her classes, never about boys (they were dumb). And although she was disciplined and tenacious in her thirst for knowledge, she also had a playful and daring spirit that thrived on adrenaline. It wasn't unusual to find her scaling a mountain, rock climbing, or bridge jumping. But because she was unassuming and humble, others would never know that she had a crazy, adventurous side. Yet if someone asked her about a recent adventure, her eyes would light up.

As we drove to the hospital, I picked up my phone and called the ER to learn about the extent of her injuries, which I assumed would calm my anxiety. I felt that if I could just talk to a doctor, he would alleviate my fears and the butterflies in my stomach would dissipate. I even imagined that they might allow me to talk with Lexi.

I was not at all prepared for what the doctor said. He informed me that a car had hit Lexi while she had been longboarding through a crosswalk on her way to class at BYU and that she had suffered a very traumatic brain injury as a result of the collision.

I gasped and pleaded with him to tell me how serious her wounds were. The doctor, hearing the panic in my voice, became concerned for my safety. He wanted to know if I was driving a vehicle before he would continue to apprise me about the extent of her injuries. I managed to keep my voice steady so that he would continue on. I don't remember everything he said, but it was obvious from what he told me that she was in a coma and that her chances of making it were slim at best. It was serious and much worse than what my husband had gathered from his short conversation with the doctor.

My pounding heart roared so loud I thought I might pass out. I couldn't fathom that this was happening to my beautiful Lexi who was good and kind and sweet to everyone. *How could she be taken from me?* I could not go on living without her bright

spirit in my life. It felt like an out-of-body experience, like it was happening to me, yet it wasn't. The searing pain, the grief, and the sorrow were all too real. It was unbearable.

I had just spoken to Lexi earlier in the day, and she was happy and full of life. She had been excited for me to watch a video of her longboarding down the scenic canyon not far from campus. She had texted me several times during the day to ask me if I had been able to watch it. Her longboard had been her means of transportation, but she also loved to longboard in the canyon to feel the wind in her face. It made her feel liberated and helped her arrange her thoughts. She was a free spirit who loved the outdoors.

And that is where my thoughts turned while we drove to the hospital; sacred memories of Lexi began to fill my mind. Tears returned afresh and trickled down my cheeks. I couldn't help but think about all the reasons I loved her.

She had always been steadfast and immovable in being obedient to the Lord's commandments. I remember many times walking into her room to find her stretched out on the floor with pen in hand, scrawling insights in her notebook that she had just gleaned from reading her

> *My soul thirsteth for God, for the living God; when shall I come and appear before God?"*
> —Psalm 42:2

scriptures. One particular day, she had been so engrossed in her studies, she had not heard me enter until I greeted her. This was her sanctuary, and it gave me a glimmer of insight into her soul. She was barely fourteen years old at the time. Glancing up, she seemed happy to see me and even more eager to talk to me.

"Mom, please don't think I'm bragging," she began. "I could only tell you this." She took a big breath and let it out, as if gaining enough courage to tell me her innermost thoughts. I had always wanted to know what deep musings were behind her face.

She continued hesitantly, "All my life I have felt different than other people. That I . . . that I have a special mission for this earth life."

Her eyes pierced mine, needing to know she could trust me with such a treasured confidence. "Ever since I was little, I knew I was here for a special reason. I feel like I see life from a totally different perspective than everyone else. I see what God wants for us. I am not bragging at all," she pleaded. "It's just a feeling I've always had."

I studied her face intently. There was such reverence in her voice. I couldn't resist bending down to reach for her hand and kissing her forehead. Perceiving now that she was safe, her eyes softened, and she continued to reveal the hidden secrets of her heart. "I have such a close relationship with God. I *know* Him!" Her voice filled with awe. A marvelous sense of peace engulfed our space and sent a shiver down my spine.

Feeling a surge of emotion, tears welled up in my eyes. I wasn't surprised by her words because I had always seen the light of heaven in her. She had a believing heart, but until now, I didn't know that *she* knew. I dropped to a crouch and wedged myself beside her and the bed, lightly running my hand through her hair before putting my arms around her neck. The Spirit was a warm friend, teaching us through the silence as a cool stream of knowledge poured into our hearts.

My Lexi was so happy and full of life. It was rare to see her without a smile on her face. I thought back to the night when I was sitting in the audience as Lexi performed a song with a choir of girls her same age. She smiled the entire performance and lit up the room with her cheerful countenance. My eyes quickly scanned the group of girls singing with her, but not one of them was smiling. Maybe they were told not to smile, but Lexi couldn't help herself. Smiling was part of who she was, a joyful, grateful, loving person that shone from the inside out.

> *A merry heart doeth good like a medicine.*
> —Proverbs 17:22

It was incomprehensible to think this light could be snuffed out, especially at such a tender age, and as a result, I didn't want to believe it. My greatest happiness in life had been my family, and I did not know how I could go on without Lexi's radiant spirit. I was in denial, but the horror of what might be started to sneak into my soul, knowing she was in such critical condition.

Just seconds after I hung up the phone with the doctor, one of my neighbors called. He had been doing a service project at the church with my husband when the hospital called, and he wanted to see if we knew yet how serious the accident was.

Although I was still in control of my emotions when I answered his call, my voice trembled as I tried to hide my fears and pain. I blurted out, "The doctors don't think that she will make it."

My voice started to crack in desperation as I tried to fight back the tears: "Please call, text, or email everyone in our church and neighborhood and have them start praying for Lexi immediately. Tell them to spread the word to their friends and family and have them pray for her as well."

After we finished our conversation, I likewise called my children who lived out of state, who had already received the news from their siblings. At the beginning of each phone call, we cried for several minutes, taking comfort in our mutual love and grief for our sweet Lexi before I could venture to say a word. Finally, while weeping and with barely an audible voice, I pleaded with them, as I had our neighbor, to call everyone they knew their extended families, friends, and neighbors so as many people as possible could call down the powers of heaven on Lexi's behalf.

Ordinarily, I am a very private person and don't often ask others for help. Yet, in this case, I knew instinctively that this was what needed to happen in order for Lexi to be healed. Because of that impression, multitudes were able to join with us in prayer and fasting for her.

In the days that followed, their faith along with ours was strengthened by the miracles that occurred. And from that moment on, I did "pray without ceasing" (1 Thessalonians: 5:17) in my heart "casting all [my cares] upon him" (1 Peter 5:7). This was the first of many promptings I received from the Spirit that let me know Lexi would recover. I know that "the Comforter, which is the Holy Ghost . . . shall teach [us to do] *all things*" (John 14:26; italics added).

Chapter Two

THE MIRACLE TO BELIEVE IN MIRACLES

The same came to Jesus by night, and said unto him, Rabbi, we know that thou art a teacher come from God: for no man can do these miracles that thou doest, except God be with him.

—John 3:2

When we arrived at the emergency room, I leaped out of the car and sprinted inside. A member of the hospital staff was waiting for me and took me directly to Lexi. Within seconds I saw her still and almost lifeless body.

Her head had begun to swell so much that others would not have recognized her, but I knew this was my Lexi. Her entire face was covered in cuts, bruises, and blood. Her lips had swollen to at least ten times their normal size. A bloodied breathing tube was in her mouth, and likewise, there was blood in and around her hair. It seemed that cords and tubes were everywhere. My eyes searched for any movement in her body.

The hospital workers shuttled in and out of the room. As I stood next to her, the truth started to sink in my mind. I was in such pain, shock, and disbelief that I felt almost numb. I gently took her hand in mine, letting her know that I was there beside her and that it would be okay. But my mind was clouded with uncertainty, allowing fear to edge its way in. I felt helpless. I was her mom; I was supposed to be able to protect my daughter. Yet here I was seemingly incapable of doing anything. But a lingering belief told me otherwise I wasn't powerless. I tried not to let go of that thought, but found it slithering away amidst the reality sitting before me. Grief poured in. And again, my mind was flooded with memories of Lexi.

It seemed like yesterday I watched Lexi bound across the lawn, a cluster of dandelions clenched in her small fist. I could still feel the press of her tiny fingers against my cheeks as she laid a kiss on my lips and handed me the treasured bouquet she had painstakingly gathered.

The memory only intensified my pain, and tightened my

fingers around her hands, believing if I clenched firmly enough,
her spirit would not slip away. I
was doing my best to hold back
my tears, but they came nonetheless. Under the crushing weight of
reality, my whole world began to
crumble. My shoulders began to

shake, and my throat constricted as the flood of tears erupted
into sobbing.

Immediately, I felt the security of McKay's arms wrapped
lovingly around me as he embraced me and held me tight. My
family would be my anchor through this trying ordeal. My son
Tanner, just two years older than Lexi, was the first to arrive at
the hospital. He had a close bond with his sister and had watched
out for her while they grew up. Seeing her in this state rocked his
world, and he felt his heart breaking. The raw, grief-stricken pain
I saw in his eyes, mingled with my own, deepened my sorrow.

Lexi's brother McKay arrived next
with his wife, Makana. He had just
returned to college to get his MBA at
the same time Lexi was starting her
first semester. He had left home when
she was only seven years old, so being
in school together had given them an
opportunity to get to know each other
better. They both played tennis in high
school, and now, after all this time and
an age gap of twelve years, they became
tennis partners for any match he could
drum up.

My daughter Kelsi was the last to arrive. To her, Lexi's body seemed strong, normal, and healthy except for her face. At the time, she remembered thinking, "Lexi is seriously hurt? Death was a possibility? That can't be true."

> Beloved, think it not strange concerning the fiery trial which is to try you, as though some strange thing happened unto you: but rejoice, inasmuch as ye are partakers of Christ's sufferings; that, when his glory shall be revealed, ye may be glad also with exceeding joy.
>
> —1 Peter 4:12–13

She couldn't wrap her head around the idea that Lexi was in a coma and wasn't able to wake up. Kelsi had never been around death or even a serious injury, and now that it was staring her in the face, she couldn't understand it. Everything was very surreal to her.

She recalled several conversations she had with her friends describing Lexi. She would boast, "My sister Lexi is one of those perfect people. She is extremely pretty, talented, smart, righteous, and kind to everyone." And then she would always add, "She is like one of those people who dies early in life because they are just too good."

Remembering her own words, Kelsi felt racked with guilt, somehow believing this was all her fault.

After a few minutes, Doug, who had been parking our car, finally joined us in the room. With our sons McKay and Tanner assisting him, he prayed over Lexi. We were only given a few minutes to be with her before we were ushered into a private room where the doctors were to meet with us.

A heavy silence followed us as we exited Lexi's room. Stares of sympathy and sadness showed in the eyes of all who met our gaze, sensing our grief. I wanted to find a place of safety and refuge, but the dark clouds of uncertainty grew ominous. I had not noticed how much noise there had been until the door shut behind us and the commotion was gone. Everywhere I looked seemed bleak and sorrowful.

In a few minutes, the doctors came in, their faces grim, and began to explain to us the grave news that Lexi had less than a one percent chance to live. I sat motionless, staring straight ahead, my eyes burning as tears continued to roll down my cheeks. At the time, I wasn't really listening. My mind was racing, and my heart was in turmoil. Everything was a blur. I kept on thinking about how this horrible accident could not have happened to my beautiful, kind Lexi. I could not lose her. Not now, not ever. In my mind, it would all turn out . . . it just had to! My heart was troubled; it was afraid (see John 14:27).

I was in a fog until my son spoke up. I heard his words loud and clear, even though he spoke in a soft tone. He asked the doctors if we needed to call family members home that were living out of state. The neurologist was empathetic and told him that we needed to call them home to Utah, and he asked how soon the family would be able to get there in order to keep Lexi alive with life support. I was in shock! I had not let my mind even consider the possibility that she might not be with us anymore. I let out a grief-stricken cry and pleaded, "Why? Why do we need to call?"

His statement had sent a fresh wave of unbelievable hurt through my heart. It was too much for my heart to bear. I had realized Lexi had some serious wounds but nothing, I thought, that couldn't heal with time. The thought had only momentarily crossed my mind that she was in such critical condition that she might not live through the night. Like Rahab, "As soon as [I] had heard these things, [my heart] did melt, neither did there remain any more courage in [me]" (Joshua 2:11). I was starting to succumb to shock as I begged the doctors, "I don't want to be here. I want to be back with my Lexi. Take me back; please take me back to my Lexi."

After hearing my heartfelt pleadings to see my daughter again, a hospital social worker named Travis jumped up from his seat and said he'd take me back to her. His eyes filled with compassion. He accompanied me back to her room in the ER and stood with me by her hospital bed. Upon viewing Lexi's lifeless body, the tears spilled out, and I started sobbing uncontrollably, my chest heaving and gasping for air.

In an effort to help me regain control, Travis began to engage me in conversation. "Were you close?" he asked, cocking his head in sympathy.

Between gasps for air, I began to haltingly speak. "She was my best friend," I said. (I am blessed to feel that way about each of my children.) "I can't lose her." There was a desperate pleading in my voice for him to tell me it would be all right, that it wasn't as bad as it seemed.

Travis continued in his attempt to calm me. "It's okay if the two of you exchanged harsh words before this," he said, thinking that was the cause of some of my pain.

I was shocked by the suggestion. "No, no. We were so close! I have no regrets." My voice seemed to beg for him to understand that she was different. She was near perfection, and a light as bright as hers could not be replaced.

"I just can't go on without her. She means everything to me," I stammered, while the tears continued to flow.

An empty hollowness burrowed its way inside of me. I needed the ray of sunshine she brought into my life. Her cheerful voice, bright smile, and countenance they were what made my life complete. I wanted Travis to know that this wasn't just a body lying there with no name. This was Lexi, my daughter. She was my joy, my life. My heart felt as if it had been ripped out of my body.

"What was she like growing up?" he asked.

I could barely speak now. "She . . . she . . . was good . . . to everyone," I whispered, my voice stifled by my tears. The enormity of all that had happened settled on me with massive force, filling my body with absolute and complete turmoil. It was the deepest anguish I had ever felt.

Travis, seeing how distraught I was, told me to take some deep breaths before I passed out. He continued to try to calm me down, but I was inconsolable.

Finally, he turned and stood in front of me, just inches away from my face, looked me directly in my eyes, and said firmly and with great intensity, "Listen, I have worked in this hospital a long time, and I have seen lots of miracles. You need to pray for a miracle. Above all, you need to know that a miracle can happen. Particularly, you need to be there for your family. They are looking to you for strength."

His words penetrated my heart. Yes, that *is* what I knew to be true! The scriptures had always been a powerful influence in my life. I had studied them daily and knew the words and the miracles I had read were true.

> And Stephen, full of faith and power, did great wonders and miracles among the people.
>
> —Acts 6:8

God is a God of miracles, and He hears and answers prayers! Yet in that small moment, I had let myself go to a place of fear and hopelessness. In seeing my daughter's lifeless body and hearing the doctors say that she wouldn't make it through the night, I'd forgotten that God knew me and that He knew Lexi. She was in His hands. He *could* heal her!

Fighting back tears, I snapped out of that state of despair and abandonment almost instantly and replaced it with an assurance, a hope and a belief that God could heal my daughter and make her whole. I began to look to God with "faith, and [to] doubt not" (Matthew: 21:21). I began to remember that "God [had] not given [me] the spirit of fear" (2 Timothy 1:7). I realized I wanted to be that rock my family could lean on.

What I was experiencing wasn't just a glimmer of hope but absolute knowledge borne of hope. Although still in anguish of soul and weighed down with what seemed the most crushing blow, I had hope. I recognized that through our humble and earnest prayers, God could heal my daughter from almost certain death if it His will that she remain with us.

I didn't get an immediate answer to such an extraordinary plea, but I knew that it would come. God had always been and would continue to be my anchor. I would give all my energy now to calling down the powers of heaven in Lexi's behalf for a miracle if that was His will. Through the depths of my despair, God filled me with inner strength.

As I hesitantly walked back to my family, I fought to stay calm. I began to muster the faith I needed for the Lord to heal my daughter, while still aching inside.

Travis looked at me and said, "I can see a change in you already."

I had humbled myself to hear his counsel. My heart was

opened, and I was able to invite the Holy Ghost back into my soul to replace my fear. I resolved to have the courage and strength I knew that my family deserved. My "eyes [could now] see afar off" (Moses 6:27). I brushed away the final tear that night with the back of my hand, telling myself to breathe slowly. I knew I must "cleave unto the Lord [my God], as [I had] done unto this day" (Joshua 23:8).

Looking back, I have pondered about that moment. I know I would have eventually come to that place of faith; however, with Travis's help, I was able to get there immediately, and for that I will be ever grateful.

> *Whosoever shall say unto this mountain, Be thou removed, and be thou cast into the sea; and shall not doubt in his heart, but shall believe that those things which he saith shall come to pass; he shall have whatsoever he saith. Therefore I say unto you, What things soever ye desire, when ye pray, believe that ye receive them, and ye shall have them.*
>
> —Mark 11:23–24

17

Chapter Three

THE MIRACLE
OF HOPE

*Blessed is the man that trusteth in the Lord, and whose hope
the Lord is.*

—Jeremiah 17:7

B ecause I had left the room to see Lexi, I had missed the doctors' explanation about the magnitude of her injuries. So, my
family gave me the details later that night.

She had contusions to her lungs, which are "bruise[s] of the lung,
caused by chest trauma. . . . The excess fluid interferes with gas
exchange, potentially leading to inadequate oxygen levels. . . . [A]
pulmonary contusion plays a key role in determining whether
an individual will die or suffer serious ill effects as the result
of trauma."[1] She also had a C2 fracture on her spinal cord.[2] A
physical therapist at the hospital later showed us a skeleton to
help us understand the severity of her injury. He told us that
a C1 fracture would result in automatic death, a C2 fracture if

broken completely would mean the patient would only be able to blink their eyes. Luckily, he said, Lexi's fracture had not broken completely, so she could have complete healing if everything went well.

However, the neurologist stated that all her physical injuries were considered minor compared to the injuries to her brain. He explained that Lexi had experienced a shearing injury in the subarachnoid area[3] of her brain as well as bleeding in either the epidural[4] or subdural[5] area. A shearing injury is when the neurons that carry electrical signals in your brain get sheared, or cut off from each other. These are vital connections in our brain that cannot be repaired once lost. And the bleeding in her brain meant that the doctors would not be able to operate. The injury was too deep, and the damage had already been done.

The physician's assistant pointed out little white specks on the CT scan and stated that these were the areas of shearing. Doug and I asked what percent chance she had of surviving.

The assistant sighed and said, "Lexi has less than a one percent chance of living, maybe two." He went on to explain that with brain injuries, they can never truly know the severity of the outcome. If Lexi were to make it, she may never walk or speak again. He said that many people who suffer brain injuries end up in a care center, never to function independently for the rest of their lives.

The neurologist then said that Lexi had been displaying "decorticate" and "decerebrate" posturing and had even been transitioning back and forth between the two.

"Abnormal posturing is an involuntary flexion or extension of the arms and legs, indicating severe brain injury. It occurs when one set of muscles becomes incapacitated while the opposing set is not, and an external stimulus such as pain causes the working set of muscles to contract. The posturing may also occur without a stimulus. Since posturing is an important indicator of the amount of damage that has occurred to the brain, it is used by medical professionals to measure the severity of a coma with the Glasgow Coma Scale (for adults) and the Pediatric Glasgow Coma Scale (for infants). The presence of abnormal posturing indicates a severe medical emergency requiring immediate medical attention. Decerebrate and decorticate posturing are strongly associated with poor outcome in a variety of conditions."[6]

Decorticate posturing is "when the patient's back arches backwards and flexes the arms, whereas decerebrate posturing is where the patient arches the back (like in decorticate posturing) but then extends the arms out parallel to the body, Both decorticate posturing and decerebrate posturing are indicative of serious head injuries with significant damage to the brain."[7] This was grave news.

I had only been back in the room with my family for a few minutes when my youngest son, Parker, opened the door and walked in with a heavy heart. He had not been at home when we had rushed to the hospital, so our next-door neighbor was kind enough to bring him. Parker had been so distraught about Lexi that he did not know if he could handle seeing her in that condition. Sensing Parker's despair, our neighbor pulled over on the side of the road to say a prayer. When our neighbor prayed, he assumed that he would pray for peace and comfort for Parker and our family, considering that from all

> The blind receive their sight, and the lame walk, the lepers are cleansed, and the deaf hear, the dead are raised up, and the poor have the gospel preached to them.
> —Matthew 11:5

accounts Lexi was not going to live. Instead, he felt impressed to ask our Heavenly Father that she would be made whole. That prayer was one of many offered for Lexi in which the Holy Ghost prompted the individual to pray for a miracle.

I was the first person Parker caught sight of when he entered the room, and he immediately burst into tears. He had been trying to be strong. His first thought was for me rather than for himself as he tried to comfort me.

Choking from emotion he said, "Mom, it's going to be okay. This earth life is minuscule when we think about eternity. It will be just a blink of an eye, and then we will be together again." He ached to have his sister with him, yet he was able to turn outward to comfort me. I was grateful that I had not let my heart give way to grief, so that I could be strong for Parker when his soul was filled with anguish.

> *Whosoever shall call on the name of the Lord shall be delivered.*
>
> —Joel 2:32

I gave him a big hug and whispered, "No, Parker, don't talk that way. We need to have faith. Lexi will be fine. She is not leaving us. We cannot lose hope." At that point, one of my favorite memorized scriptures came to mind. "And this is the confidence that we have in him, that, if we ask any thing according to his will, he heareth us" (1 John 5:14). Knowing I was in God's hands and knowing that He has all power helped remove my fear.

Being a pillar of strength and faith for my son would have been impossible minutes earlier. But now I felt "troubled on every side, yet not distressed . . . perplexed, but not in despair; Persecuted, but not forsaken; cast down, but not destroyed" (2 Corinthians 4:8–9).

After this exchange with Parker, my husband and I were able

to call our children living out of state. We asked them to join with us over speaker phone as we knelt for a family prayer on behalf of Lexi. From the deepest and most tender part of my soul, I pleaded to God that He would hear a mother's prayer on behalf of her daughter and heal Lexi just as the Savior had raised Lazarus from the dead. Every thought and every spoken word was directed heavenward for a divine answer.

Although it felt much longer, it had been just over an hour since we received the call to come to the hospital. I felt like I was standing at the base of a steep mountain of adversity. Little did I know how rugged the journey to the peak would be and how long it would take to discover if God would allow a miracle to happen for Lexi. But I could feel the wind at my back, pushing me upward on the rocky incline. I knew there would be more soul stretching in the hours and days ahead. As Job, I knew that God could "do every *thing*" (Job 42:2; italics added), "for the eyes of the Lord *are over* the righteous, and his ears *are open* unto their prayers" (1 Peter 3:12; italics added).

NOTES

1. *Wikipedia*, s.v. "Pulmonary Contusion," last updated October 6, 2017, https://en.wikipedia.org/wiki/Pulmonary_contusion.

2. A C2 fracture is a fracture on the second vertebra of the spine. The C-spine is the "most feared of all spinal injuries . . . [and] the higher the level of the C-spine injury, the higher the morbidity and mortality" (Igor Boyarsky, "C2 Fractures," *Medscape*, last updated February 2, 2017, https://emedicine.medscape.com /article/1267150-overview).

3. The subarachnoid space is a small space on the surface of the hemispheres of the brain and is filled with spongy connective tissue and "intercommunicating channels in which the cerebrospinal fluid is contained" (*Wikipedia*, s.v. "Subarachnoid Space," last modified May 1, 2017, https://en.wikipedia.org/wiki /Subarachnoid-space).

4. The epidural space is the outermost part of the spinal canal. "In humans the epidural space contains lymphatics, spinal nerve roots, loose connective tissue, fatty tissue, small arteries, and a network of internal vertebral venous plexuses" (*Wikipedia*, s.v. "Epidural Space," last modified June 12, 2015, https://en.wikipedia.org/wiki /Epidural-space).

5. The subdural space is a "potential space" that can be created by an injury (*Wikipedia*, s.v. "Subdural Space," last modified March 26, 2017, https://en.wikipedia.org/wiki/Subdural_space).

6. *Wikipedia*, s.v. "Abnormal Posturing," last modified March 4, 2017, https://en.wikipedia.org/wiki/Abnormal_posturing.

7. "What Is the Difference between Decorticate and Decerebrate Posturing?" *Emergency Medical Paramedic*, accessed October 31, 2017, http://www.emergencymedicalparamedic.com/what-is-the -difference-between-decorticate-and-decerebrate-posturing.

Chapter Four

THE MIRACLE OF A GRATEFUL HEART

In every thing give thanks.

—1 Thessalonians 5:18

After our family prayer, I suggested that each of us individually kneel down and say a silent prayer of gratitude. I believe that there is great power in gratitude prayers. While I prayed, I pondered on the many instances where Lexi had shown thanksgiving. Hers was a soul overflowing with appreciation, especially when it came to God's creations. I wistfully reflected on the last evening she was at home.

"Mom, did you see the sunset?" Lexi asked breathlessly as she came running in the house to make sure I didn't miss it. "It's spectacular!" she said in earnest, flashing a smile at me.

I hurried to the window and saw the most brilliant reds and oranges painting the canvas of the sky in a fiery display. As the sun receded behind the mountain, the wave of colors still lingered as if accidentally left behind. Lexi was spellbound, as if it were the first time she'd seen the splendor of the setting sun. She never lost her enthusiasm for the nightly event. Each new sunset became her favorite. I loved that about Lexi; she was always on the lookout for goodness.

> *It is not happy people who are thankful. It is thankful people who are happy.*
> —Unknown Author

Lexi's gratitude was contagious because she was happy. My mind continued to sift through the sweet memories; image after image sprang to my mind.

For example, one cool and crisp fall morning, when the trees were sporting new autumn colors of red and yellow, Lexi couldn't resist the temptation of calling out to her brothers to come help as she ran to grab a rake. Our yard was a sea of leaves, and

she couldn't believe her good fortune. Within an hour, I heard her contagious laugh and hurried outside to join in the festivities. I knew whatever they had been up to would prove to be fun. There was always a spontaneous energy about her.

Under the big globe willow tree was a massive pile of leaves they had worked hard to create. I stepped outside just in time to see Lexi leaning forward out of the tree, squinting up at the sun before she sailed out of the safety of its branches into the enormous mountain of crusty brown and orange leaves gleaming in the sunlight. Laughing hysterically, leaves poking from her hair, she threw up a handful of leaves in the air before calling out, asking Parker to jump.

The sniffles from family members brought my thoughts back to reality and back to the hospital, and the pain pierced through me once again. I needed to focus, to remember her goodness, to let the Lord know I was thankful for what was now eighteen very short years. Glancing up, I saw a few of my children getting up off their knees, but I didn't want to stop praying just yet. I retreated back into my thoughts.

Lexi's own gratitude was evident at an early age. I thought of a treasured memory. When she was just seven years old, she had lost a tooth and was so excited for the tooth fairy to come. I assumed it was to get money.

Cease not to give thanks.
—Ephesians 1:16

That night, when the last of daylight had faded away, I crept into her room and knelt by her bed to put some coins under her pillow. Much to my surprise, I found a sweet note addressed to the tooth fairy, some coins, and a miniature tea set. In the note, she thanked the tooth fairy for being so kind to all the boys and girls in the world by giving them money for their teeth. She continued by explaining that she knew the tooth fairy must be tired, so the tea set was there for her to relax and take a break. Lexi wrote that she didn't want any money for her tooth but instead wanted to give the tooth fairy money so she would not have to work as hard. Lexi had very little money at that age and had given every last coin to the tooth fairy.

Then another recollection came so vividly; I felt I could reach out and touch it as it happened. It was a warm spring day when dark gray clouds gathered in the sky, releasing a sudden shower. The downpour pelted our roof, startling everyone inside. Not one to feel cooped up, Lexi squealed with delight as she scampered out the door, barefoot, with the rest of her siblings, not hesitating a moment.

Forming a line, they zigzagged, jumped, and twirled, following the leader of the pack's every move. Rain trickled down their faces as they stomped in fresh pools of water, relishing every second of the downpour. A smile stole across Lexi's face. She saw every kind of storm as a blessing in disguise. I wished to go back in time if just for a day to feel her love and gratitude.

I continued to pray. How could I not be thankful for the time I had with her? I was a better person in her presence because she made me feel of worth. She never expected anything, even on her birthday. In fact, she would specifically ask me not to give her a present. And no matter how small the gift or gesture, her appreciation knew no bounds.

I thought about the times I would invariably find a note on my pillow from her, thanking me for the fun trip after we came home from a vacation. Even though our trips weren't exotic, she never felt slighted that we couldn't spend much on them. Lexi was a giver. She had a warmth about her that made others feel comfortable. Neighbors and friends were surprised to find notes in their mailboxes, thanking them for service they had given to her or to others.

My heart continued to swell while I pondered Lexi's spirit. While each member of the family spent some time on their knees, thanking Heavenly Father for blessings, a feeling of love and humility came over all of us, and we knew that the Lord was in charge. After those tender moments of expressing gratitude to our Father in Heaven, I felt a greater outpouring of the spirit. Eventually, I was pulled away from my wistful musings and got up off my knees.

We had finished our gratitude prayers, and an employee came in to tell us they had seen a "hint of life" in Lexi, and they were going to move her upstairs to the Intensive Care Unit (ICU). What a powerful testimony to our family of the power of prayer! It was immediately after we finished our petitions that her chance of survival went from almost zero percent to one percent. We realized later that if we had not offered those prayers, she would not be with us now.

GRATITUDE CHANGED MY FAMILY

Looking back on this family prayer experience, I realize that saying a prayer of thanks wouldn't have entered my mind if it weren't for a tender mercy given to me a month before the accident. While I was saying my nightly prayer, I had the distinct impression to start speaking only gratitude prayers. Morning and evening, individual and family petitions became communions with God to acknowledge everything He had given me.

At first, when I began the practice of only thanking God for blessings, it was hard not to sneak in a favor that was desperately needed. It was particularly difficult not to ask the Lord to help my children. After all, one daughter was struggling to get pregnant, and a son was in need of a job. However, in time I grew in spiritual wisdom, and I stopped struggling to only pray with thanksgiving. I felt calm and peaceful, in contrast to prayers of pleading and desperation, and I began to find that I was more receptive to the whisperings of the Holy Spirit. I came to understand that gratitude brought benefits to my life that I was not fully aware of until later.

> *I thank my God always on your behalf.*
> —1 Corinthians 1:4

Instead of asking for my daughter to get pregnant, I learned to say thank you for a beautiful daughter who remained faithful and steadfast despite not being able to bear a child. And I was able to give thanks for a son who trusted in God's plan for him despite not finding a job. It changed my whole perspective as I prayed with thanksgiving. I began to see God's grace unfold in my life instead of seeing petitions go unanswered. Developing this habit before the accident made it second nature to give a prayer of gratitude at the hospital.

The scriptures teach, "Behold, I have refined thee, but not with silver; I have chosen thee in the furnace of affliction" (Isaiah 48:10). "And even to your old age I am he; and even to hoar hairs will I carry you: I have made, and I will bear; even I will carry, and will deliver you" (Isaiah 46:4)

We had the opportunity to tell Lexi's story many times. On one occasion, while being interviewed, I felt impressed to include the experience of gratitude prayers. I hoped that others might be inspired to express more appreciation in their prayers. As I was telling a reporter our experience, she stopped me to ask what a gratitude prayer was. As I explained what kind of prayer that would entail, she was incredulous. She didn't believe that anyone could give a prayer of gratitude while their daughter lay in a coma in the emergency room. And with all things considered, she assumed her readers would not believe me either.

Now will I praise the Lord.
—Genesis 29:35

She asked, "What in the world did you pray for at that difficult moment in time?"

I explained that I thanked my Father in Heaven for the eighteen years that he'd allowed me to have with my daughter. I thanked him particularly for her goodness, for her love for the Lord, for her bright and happy spirit, and for her light. I likewise thanked him for my other children, as well as for their good lives that reflected God's kindness to everyone they met. I thanked Him for my Savior, who is the great Healer, for His atoning sacrifice, and for His anguish in Gethsemane that allowed Him to understand my suffering in that minute. In short, I told the reporter that I knew there was great power in gratitude prayers, despite what most people may believe.

Among many reasons, I believe one reason Lexi is still here with us today is because God blesses those who recognize His kindness and who focus on what others have done for them and not solely on their own selfish desires. He wanted to teach me a lesson, and for that I will always be thankful. Acknowledging God's hand in my life has changed me.

There are scriptural accounts that exemplify the power of gratitude. Who is not touched by the power of Job's gratitude for the Lord when he is stricken with afflictions on every front? Job's property, camels, sheep, oxen, and his children are destroyed. Yet when he was informed of these tragedies, he said, "Naked came I out of my mother's womb, and naked shall I return thither: the Lord gave, and the Lord hath taken away; blessed be the name of the Lord" (Job 1:21). Job's ability to give thanks to God when all was taken from him; resulted in "the Lord giving Job twice as much as he had before" (Job 42:10). I do not doubt that it was Job's ability to give thanks that allowed Job to have such spiritual power.

Another account I love is that of the prophet Daniel in the Old Testament. In his day, a decree went forth throughout the kingdom stating that no one was permitted to pray, or they would be killed. After learning of this law, Daniel "went into his house; and his windows being open . . . he kneeled upon his knees three times a day, and prayed, and gave *thanks* before his God, as he did aforetime" (Daniel 6:10; italics added).

Because Daniel disobeyed the king's command, he was taken to the lion's den to be killed. But Daniel explains, "God hath sent his angel, and hath shut the lions' mouths, that they have not hurt me" (Daniel 6:22). Can we not attribute Daniel's miraculous escape from the lion's den to the prayers of gratitude he had offered up? Fasting was also part of this miracle (and we will soon see that it will also be a part of Lexi's miracle). The scriptures explain that after Daniel was cast into the den of lions, The king went to his palace, and passed the night fasting" (Daniel 6:18).

> As he entered into a certain village, there met him ten men that were lepers. . . . And they lifted up their voices, and said, Jesus, Master, have mercy on us. And when he saw them, he said unto them, Go shew yourselves unto the priests. . . . As they went, they were cleansed. And one of them, when he saw that he was healed, turned back, and with a loud voice glorified God, and fell down on his face at his feet, giving him thanks.
>
> —Luke 17:12–16

As I have looked back on this experience, I stand in awe at how quickly the Lord answered our pleadings for Lexi. My testimony in the power of prayer increased greatly especially in gratitude prayers. God does hear us. He wants to bless us and will pour out as many blessings upon our heads as we are ready to accept. He is waiting for us to come to Him for help.

The beginning of Lexi's miracle had commenced, and every family member was a literal witness of God's power to heal and change an outcome that seemed to have already been decided by doctors and science. We learned for ourselves that to such an extent that we "seek the Lord God . . . with all [our] heart and all [our] soul . . . and with [our] whole desire . . . he [is] found of [us]" (2 Chronicles 15:12, 15).

Chapter Five

THE MIRACLE OF CHRIST'S HEALING POWER OF FORGIVENESS

And be ye kind one to another, tenderhearted, forgiving one another, even as God for Christ's sake hath forgiven you.

—Ephesians 4:32

When we walked into the hallway to go upstairs to the ICU, I saw a group of Lexi's friends huddled together in the corridor, somber and full of anxiety. Word had spread rapidly on social media of Lexi's accident, and they had rushed directly over to the hospital, waiting desperately for any information on her status.

I wanted to encircle my arms around them and console them. I could see the grief and despair in their faces. But the glass doors slid open, and an EMT came walking in the building, carrying Lexi's backpack and the two broken pieces of her longboard.

My heart quickened with dread. Seeing her damaged longboard pierced my soul and made me physically ill at a time when I didn't think my pain could grow any worse. Yet somehow it did.

I abruptly looked the other way and stared silently at the wall to avoid looking at her personal possessions. I tried to drown out the image that had filled my mind, perceiving I would collapse if I gave into my feelings. In a daze, I followed the assistant upstairs, where my family was led to a waiting area on the floor of the ICU.

During this time, my son McKay and my daughter-in-law Makana drove to the scene of the accident in hopes of finding the driver of the car that hit Lexi to make sure that he was okay. I was caught off guard when one of the first things McKay said to me after we saw Lexi's body was that our family needed to go check on the driver. The world had come crashing down on us, and yet he was able to look beyond our harsh surroundings to someone else's plight.

I was still in shock, trying to awake from my awful nightmare, and I found it extraordinary that he had the presence of mind to think of the driver at that horrifying moment. Each of us knew the torment the driver must have been going through, realizing that he might have killed someone; we wanted to make sure he was okay. All I could muster was a nod of my head, but inside I was pleased that the driver had not been forgotten in his time of need.

Regrettably, he was gone by the time my son and his wife got there. And the driver told us later that he was actually worried that we would try to

> *And forgiving one another . . . even as Christ forgave you, so also do ye.*
>
> —1 Corinthians 3:13

find him and was relieved that he was allowed to leave the scene before we got there.

As I reflected on this experience later, I realized that McKay's and Makana's reactions were like that of Rebekah in the book of Genesis. Abraham had asked his servant to find a wife for his son Isaac. Upon arriving in the city of Nahor with ten camels, this servant saw a damsel by a well. He said, "Let me, I pray thee, drink a little water of thy pitcher" (Genesis 24:17). Instead of being upset that he would ask her to do something he could do himself, "she hasted, and let down her pitcher upon her hand, and gave him drink. And when she had done giving him drink . . . [she] ran again unto the well to draw water, and drew for all his camels" (Genesis 24:18, 20).

I love Rebekah's response. She doesn't complain and say it was a hard thing that she was required to do, but instead, the record states that "she hasted." Her gait showed a woman that was joyful to have the opportunity to serve and to follow Christ's teachings that "whatsoever ye would that men should do to you, do ye even so to them" (Matthew 7:12).

That was exactly the reaction of my son and daughter-in-law when they received the horrible news that our precious Lexi had no chance of survival. They "hasted" back to the scene of the accident to find the driver and to console him. They knew instinctively to love and to forgive, as Rebekah instinctively knew to love. They didn't put limits on their compassion by making excuses or holding a grudge until the offending party apologized.

They could easily have said in their hearts that forgiveness was all well and good but did not apply in this situation because it involved their sister, whom they loved and admired. Was our family really supposed to forgive the person who might have killed Lexi?

Gratefully, our entire family felt the same way: we wanted to let the driver know of our love and to follow the scriptural admonition, "For if ye forgive men their trespasses, your heavenly Father will also forgive you: But if ye forgive not men their trespasses, neither will your Father forgive your trespasses" (Matthew 6:14–15).

Is this not a greater miracle? The ability to forgive and to love unconditionally? Do we sometimes mistakenly believe that the offending party needs to come to us and ask for forgiveness before we can forgive them? Forgiveness brings healing both to those who are forgiven and also to those who absolve them of their guilt, thus bringing respite to both.

We sat and prayed silently in the waiting room while they were stitching up Lexi's face in the ICU. I knew that I couldn't supplicate the Lord with a great petition unless I was kneeling. I felt I needed to give the God of this universe, He who gives sight to the blind and healing to the lame and the breath of life to my daughter, my utmost respect and devotion. It might seem like a small thing, but I knew of no other way to approach a being that could restore life to the dead than to kneel, even though it meant doing so in a very public place. With these thoughts in mind, I found a corner of the waiting room and knelt in prayer. I pleaded with God to know His will for Lexi. Would my heart be strong enough to bear the coming test? I needed to "come boldly unto the throne of grace to help [me in this] time of need" (Hebrews 4:16).

> *Casting all your care upon him; for he careth for you.*
>
> —1 Peter 5:7

As I continued to pray in my heart, my siblings arrived and gave me support with expressions of love and faith. My brother told me of his own intercessory prayer on my behalf. He explained to the Lord that I was a good and faithful woman of God and that I was worthy to have my petitions for my daughter answered. Oh, how those words touched me and gave me courage! It was priceless to know that I had nothing to hide, no great sins that would keep me from asking for God's healing touch to renew Lexi's body and bring her back whole and well. I also knew of my brother's great faith and felt that if anyone could pray for heaven's help on my behalf, he could. My son Tanner similarly whispered comfort as he bore his testimony to me. I needed his testimony, as it was a reminder to me that the Redeemer is the giver of life.

When they had finished stitching up Lexi's face, a nurse's voice jarred my mind back to the present as she asked me and my husband to follow her to Lexi's room. As I stood up to go, I could barely move my feet one in front of the other. My body seemed to be shutting down, and my legs refused to obey me. It was as if I were walking through quick sand.

Shuffling down the corridor, we finally reached her room. We were only allowed to stay for a couple of minutes before we were ushered again into the waiting room. As the doors swung open wide, I tried again to move my legs but couldn't. I was immobilized, too weak to support myself. It was a surreal experience.

Without saying a word, my brothers knew instinctively that I needed aid and hurried to my side. Taking arm, they assisted me to a nearby chair, where I subsequently collapsed. Seeing what bad shape I was in, they asked if I would like a blessing. Tanner offered to be the mouthpiece for God.

"Certainly I will be with thee," (Exodus 3:12) is the message that I felt as Tanner spoke words from our Father in Heaven.

Not just that God would be with me, which would be powerful in and of itself, but that God would *certainly* ensure there would be no confusion about His loyalty. He would be the source of my strength. It was a beautiful blessing and gave me the added fortitude that my heart and spirit needed to get through what would be a long and sleepless night.

Would the God of miracles choose in His great knowledge and wisdom to make Lexi whole? I was haunted by the unknown. And I had no idea of the intense and gut-wrenching struggle still ahead of me. I would need to reach to the very ends of my soul to know what God's desire for our family would be, but one thing I did know was that *He* could give us a miracle.

After the blessing, I gathered all the physical strength I could muster, because my husband and I were summoned once again to go back into Lexi's room. As we entered, a nurse was upset that we had come in the wrong door from the waiting area; she immediately started to scold us. I stood in stunned silence at her rebuke, while the physician's assistant promptly told her that he was to blame because he had asked us to follow him. The nurse gave me a smoldering look and with self-righteous indignation continued to get after us. "You shouldn't have gone this way," she said coldly.

I was totally caught off guard. It had only been a few hours since Lexi's accident. I was still in severe shock and filled with overwhelming heartache. Yet we were getting rebuked for the most trivial of actions. The conversation wasn't worth engaging in, but I couldn't take her flippant attitude anymore and said calmly but firmly, "Seriously? You are getting after me for going in the wrong door while my daughter is lying here in front of you, near death?"

She squirmed a little at my temperate rebuke, but it only

made her dig in her heels more and repeat like a drill sergeant the importance of going through the right door. I blew out a breath in exasperation. I was dumbfounded at the lack of compassion she had for us.

As the physician's assistant left the room, I followed after him and asked him if he could get us a new nurse. I told him I knew that the only way Lexi would be healed was by angels, but they would not come in a room filled with contention. I was surprised by my own words. I had never thought about asking for angels to help because I had the Holy Ghost to guide and direct me. Yet the impression had come forcefully to my mind. It was absolutely clear to me that angels would be invaluable for her survival.

The physician's assistant explained to me that this nurse was one of the best on the floor and that I wouldn't want to switch her. Upon hearing this, I realized that her expertise would also be an essential part in Lexi's survival. I needed to turn this unpleasant experience into a good one; I needed to become her friend in order to have heaven's help. So I returned to the room with an open heart and inquired about her family and interests, despite my own grief. The corners of her mouth softened, and although she never apologized, it wasn't long before the room was filled with warmth. With the previous tension gone, I realized I had survived this encounter. Forgiving the nurse now freed me to focus on Lexi.

It was a harsh reality to learn that despite the grief I was experiencing, there would be those who would add to my cloud of despair instead of looking for ways to take my pain away. I wondered how many times I had made this same mistake by letting pride get in the way of charity just to prove a point or allowing the letter of the law to distract me from things that mattered more.

I was able to reach out to this nurse in kindness when I saw her as a child of God. I tried to envision what she might be going through in her own life. Did she have pressing problems of her own that might have caused her to lash out at me? When I recognized these other possibilities, her jarring words no longer held their sting.

I have always enjoyed reading the final part of the story of Joseph of Egypt. Because of a famine in all the land, Joseph's brothers had traveled to Egypt to buy grain. However, they had no idea that the person they were negotiating with was their brother. I become emotional each time I read where Joseph reveals himself to his brothers, reassuring them of his love and forgiveness. He declares, "Be not grieved, nor angry with yourselves, that ye sold me hither: for God did send me before you to preserve life" (Genesis 45:5). Joseph showed compassion and tenderness instead of exacting revenge, and we love him for it. As I began to show the nurse charity, my heart changed, and I felt only love for her. Just as I knew that forgiving the nurse and the driver was paramount to having the faith necessary for a miracle, so it is in our daily walk of life. God's power will be magnified as we quickly forgive.

> For what glory is it, if, when ye be buffeted for your faults, ye shall take it patiently? But if, when ye do well, and suffer for it, ye take it patiently, this is acceptable with God.
>
> —1 Peter 2:20

Chapter Six

THE MIRACLE OF GOD'S POWER

But ye are a chosen generation, a royal priesthood, an holy nation, a peculiar people; that ye should shew forth the praises of him who hath called you out of darkness into his marvelous light.

—1 Peter 2:9

Shortly after Doug and I were permitted to come back into Lexi's room, they allowed the rest of the family to do so as well. Usually they don't allow large groups to congregate in the ICU, but I'm sure they allowed all of us to be there together that night because they didn't believe Lexi would live until morning.

Clutching the rail of her bed with one hand while gripping fiercely to Makana's hand with the other, I felt momentary relief. Yet inside me, I could feel a volcano of pain erupting again. I stared expressionless at Lexi but continued to squeeze tighter and tighter, hoping the crush of my hands could alleviate my anguish.

As I stared at her, I knew she could come through this. She had always been tough. I thought back to a tennis match of hers I watched years ago. Lexi was a natural—agile and quick. She was on fire, rocketing volleys with perfect timing.

The first time she had picked up a tennis racket, she could hit with her back hand with the same precision and power as her right hand, something rarely seen. But she was still very motivated to practice, setting high goals for herself. When the sun peeked over the mountain, she was up, riding her bike to the courts. In the evening, she would continue to develop her stroke and top spin by hammering the ball against our garage door hundreds of times, every stroke deliberate, until her arm became sore. The throbbing pain in her elbow would sometimes become so excruciating she couldn't play.

Her serve was near perfection, one of the best in the state, the toss high and forward. Then wham! another precise placement, making her opponent scramble for the ball or, more often, resulting in another ace. It wasn't unusual for Lexi to even beat some of the boys' varsity team players. She was a fierce competitor and would dart across the court, diving for a ball and scraping her elbows and knees in the process, sacrificing her body for a point.

The beeping of the machine startled me. I glanced up, and across from me stood Tanner. Instantly, I felt the impression that he should give Lexi a blessing, although she had already been given one in the ER. I knew that the sacred healing power we receive when we "call for the elders of the church; and [have] them pray over [the sick], anointing [them] with oil in the name of the Lord" (James 5:14) was another aspect that was needed to make Lexi whole.

I had great faith in each of the men in my family and in their ability to receive inspiration to know the mind and will of God and to have the heavens opened to them. I knew personally of the miracles that occur as men speak what God would say if He were present. Would God inspire the worthy men in our family as they prayed over Lexi to make her whole?

> Is any sick among you? Let him call for the elders of the church; and let them pray over him, anointing him with oil in the name of the Lord: And the prayer of faith shall save the sick, and the Lord shall raise him up.
>
> —James 5:14

Tanner describes his feelings as he prayed over Lexi in this way:

On the night of the accident I had the strong impression that I needed to give Lexi a prayer of healing. However, I knew that I was lacking the faith necessary to do it. I felt just as the father with the child possessed by the evil spirit did in Mark 9:23–24: "Jesus said unto him, If thou canst believe, all things are possible to him that believeth. And straightway the father of the child cried out, and said with tears, Lord, I believe; help thou mine unbelief."

I also felt like Jarius in Mark 5:22–23, 35–36: "And, behold, there cometh one of the rulers of the synagogue, Jairus by name; and when he saw him, he fell at his feet, And besought him greatly, saying, My little daughter lieth at the point of death: I pray thee, come and lay thy hands on her, that she may be healed; and she shall live. . . . While he yet spake, there came from the ruler of the synagogue's house certain which said, Thy daughter is dead: why troublest thou the Master any further? As soon as Jesus heard the word that was spoken, he saith unto the ruler of the synagogue, Be not afraid, only believe."

Just like this father, I pleaded with the Lord to help me have the faith to believe that a miracle could come forth. As I prayed, I felt the Lord strengthening me so I, too, could believe. And although I was given the strength to believe, I still had to act, and that was the hardest part.

When we finally got to see Lexi, a wave of emotion and fear overcame me as I saw what state she was in. But the Lord did not fail me; he truly lifted me and strengthened my faith at a time when I needed to have the courage to give my sister a blessing of healing. "As I laid my hands upon her head, I felt confidence in the Lord through the Sprit that she would be healed. As I spoke, the words that came were not my own but were the words of God. These words, 'Be not unbelieving, but only believe,' and 'through the Atonement of Jesus Christ, she will be healed,' still ring in my ears today and bring me great comfort and peace. At that moment, I knew without a doubt that she would be healed through Him. The sacredness of the prayer cannot fully be expressed, but, in that moment, I knew without a doubt that the power of Christ was real.

I have pondered on those words, "Through the Atonement of Jesus Christ, she will be healed," many times. I knew that this healing process she would go through would be long and difficult, just like it is in our lives at times. But I also know that, just like Lexi, we can be healed not only physically but also spiritually through Him as well. The power of God is real! I know that Christ lives—there is no doubt in my mind. I testify of His power and love. I love Him; He is my Savior and King, and through Him we can all be healed."

This prayer was a direct answer to our family that God would heal Lexi if we exhibited enough faith in Him so that He could accomplish His grand design in our family's behalf.

Tanner continued:

Since day one of Lexi's accident, my mom had the impression from the Holy Ghost that we should pray over Lexi through the laying on of hands every day in order for her to continue to progress. On top of that, my mom also made sure we were always wearing a white shirt and tie, as it symbolizes cleanliness and power. I watched as my brothers, father, and brothers-in-law each prepared through fasting and prayer before they laid their hands on Lexi in order for her to receive God's favor and protection.

We truly saw the huge impact it had on Lexi and her progress when we gave her a blessing of healing. Each time she was blessed, the room was immediately filled with the Spirit, and we felt the presence of angels in the room, strengthening her. Not only did Lexi start to heal, but our own faith was subsequently strengthened as we prepared for these blessings. Each grace that was pronounced was an added witness that she would be made whole and restored to her health completely.

A few times when we forgot to give her a blessing, there was a noticeable difference, as Lexi struggled a lot more in her progress. As a result, my mom would hurry and call one of us to pray over her, and then she would start to improve again.

We heard the voice of God and felt His power and ability to heal Lexi. We knew that God was perfectly aware of the situations we were in. How grateful we were then and are now for a loving Heavenly Father who has provided us with the scriptures to bring us knowledge of His plan for us and comfort in our time of need. Although only one formal prayer is needed after an accident or illness, as Tanner mentioned, I had a strong impression that Lexi needed to "receive the blessing from the Lord" (Psalm 24:5) every day. A couple of family members reminded me that this wasn't necessary, but I couldn't deny the spiritual prompting I felt to do this. In fact, as soon as my husband and sons walked in Lexi's room wearing their white shirts and ties, I felt a power overshadow me, much like the people in Peter's day felt when he walked the streets. Because of Peter's extraordinary faith and exact obedience, the believing brought the sick into the streets on beds "that at the least the shadow of Peter passing by might overshadow some of them. . . . and they were healed every one" (Acts 5:15–16).

There cannot be power given from heaven unless mortal men are clean, worthy, ready, and righteous, as Peter was, so that God can speak through them. For those "full of faith and power, did great wonders and miracles among the people" (Acts 6:8).

I was grateful to know I could ask any of the men in my family to pray over her and know they were pure and prepared in every way spiritually to use the gift given to them. They had taken to heart the words of Joshua when he said, "Sanctify yourselves: for to morrow the Lord will do wonders among you" (Joshua 3:5). We never know when our faith will be needed, so we should always be watchful and prayerful.

Chapter Seven

THE MIRACLE TO KNOW
THE WILL OF GOD

*I have trodden the winepress alone; and of the people there
was none with me . . . I looked, and there was none to help;
and I wondered that there was none to uphold.*

—Isaiah 63:3, 5

The night of Lexi's accident was the longest night of my life. I was heartbroken and devastated, staggering under a load of grief. Even though I had been reminded and knew deep within my heart that God could perform a miracle—and that Tanner, standing in as God's spokesman, had pronounced a blessing on her head that she would be healed—I had not received that witness from the Holy Ghost myself.

Looking back, I believe that the Lord had some things to teach me about suffering and about faith. I knew of Tanner's faith, and it had strengthened mine. But I also knew this blessing could not be realized without absolute faith on our family's part

51

during this dark and terrible hour. Could we walk the bitter path of discipleship? I was shaken to the very core of my being, realizing that Lexi could be taken away from me. More than anything else, I needed to know God's will for myself.

There was a clock above Lexi's bed that I looked at frequently, praying for the hours to go by quickly so that the nightmare would end, and I could take my daughter home. Instead, time seemed to stand still as the night dragged on and on. While I sat by her bed, holding her hand between mine, the grief and suffering were unbearable. I decided that I would not look at the clock again until I knew that an hour had gone by. When what seemed like an eternity had passed, I eagerly looked up at the clock, knowing that I had erased away some dreadful moments of time. To my dismay, only two minutes had gone by! I couldn't understand how that could be possible. I knew that I had sat there for at least two hours. I said to myself, "Is it possible that the clock is wrong? How am I going to make it through this night?"

The Lord's promise to us is, "I will not leave you comfortless," (John 14:18) yet I felt no comfort. He said, "Peace I give unto you," (John 14:27) yet I felt no peace. I'd never prayed, suffered, and struggled with more intensity in my life. When would the sun appear, ending the agony of the night? It was as if the Lord was lengthening the time in order that I might understand, in a small way, His own suffering. I closed my eyes and said another silent prayer, letting a pained groan escape. I breathed deeply, every second excruciating to live through.

Finally, the morning did come, but it did not bring the relief I was expecting. That day

> *Hath God forgotten to be gracious? Hath he in anger shut up his tender mercies?*
>
> —Psalm 77:9

passed by just as slowly. I had "cried unto the Lord in [my] trouble." (Psalm 107:6).

As I sat by Lexi's bed hour after hour, holding her hand, feeling her spirit, I had a lot of time to reflect. One thing I realized was that the Lord was in this experience before the accident even happened.

The morning before Lexi was hit, I had been preparing for the lesson I was supposed to teach in my church on Abraham sacrificing his son Isaac. As I studied for the lesson, I was prompted to listen to a podcast called *Enduring It Well*. I had discovered

> No matter how serious the trial, how deep the distress, how great the affliction, [God] will never desert us. He never has, and He never will. He cannot do it. It is not His character [to do so]. He is an unchangeable being; the same yesterday, the same today, and He will be the same throughout the eternal ages to come. We have found that God. We have made Him our friend, by obeying His Gospel; and He will stand by us. We may pass through the fiery furnace; we may pass through deep waters; but we shall not be consumed nor overwhelmed. We shall emerge from all these trials and difficulties the better and purer for them, if we only trust in our God and keep His commandments.
>
> —George Q. Cannon[1]

this series for the first time when I had been looking for a modern-day example of Abraham and Isaac.

I clicked on the podcast and listened to a story about a family that had lost a child to a disease. I was deeply touched by their faith. I was mesmerized as I listened to how they dealt with their shock, sorrow, and gloom by turning to the Savior. They related how they coped with their new reality, their sorrow, and the dramatic change in their lives by trusting in God's plan for them and their loved one.

I continued to listen to story after story on this station while I did chores around the house, fighting my emotions because of the unbelievable, heart-wrenching stories.

Deep within my soul, I desired to be like these individuals and families. Could I also not waver, no matter the amount of adversity thrown my way? In my time of trouble, could I "turn unto the Lord God of Israel, and [seek] him," knowing "he [would be] found" (2 Chronicles 15:4)?

These stories were so inspiring that I called two of my daughters living out of state to tell them what I had learned. I found it incredible that families who had lost loved ones and individuals who had lost limbs or been paralyzed could feel such peace and understanding. But more than anything, I sorrowed for their pain and their loss. I felt sure that a death or a similar tragedy would not happen to me because I could barely listen to the heartbreaking stories of total strangers. They had experienced what most of us have hoped never to experience. I figured God knew me well enough to know I could not handle a sorrow of such magnitude. He knew what I could bear.

A specific idea mentioned in the podcast stood out to me: it was one thing to say you will have faith when something bad happens to you, but it is another thing altogether to actually live through and experience a trial firsthand. Only then will you know whether or not your faith is strong enough not to waver. How much faith do you really possess?

Each person interviewed reiterated the point that faith in God really means having trust in God. Can you trust that God knows what is best for you even though you don't like the outcome?

I continued to listen to these real-life examples as I prepared for my lesson on Sunday, not realizing that I would never teach that lesson. Instead, I would be called upon to *live* that lesson. Would I be strong enough to apply those principles in my own life? Would I trust God?

I soon found that what these families said was true. My faith needed to be strengthened. When the shock, pain, and absolute trauma of the experience seemed too much to bear, one of the first things that came to my mind was the words of these individuals on the podcast series, "Faith means trusting the Lord." It was one of the many loving mercies given to me. I was reminded that God knew me and that I must trust in what *His* plan for me would be. I had no need to be afraid, for God was "with [me] to deliver [me]" (Jeremiah 1:8). I let those words sink in.

I knew Jesus had opened the eyes of the blind and healed the sick. He could also heal Lexi. And I knew He could carry me through this experience because He had already borne my anguish and despair. I wanted Him to silence my aching heart. I knew His was the only well I could drink from. I tried to keep that thought in the forefront of my mind. Now was the time to prove that my faith was unwavering, that I *would* trust God no matter the outcome.

But still I needed to know what the Lord's desire was for Lexi. Was it God's will that her life be extended? I took deep breaths, continuing to reach heavenward with my thoughts and prayers. I knew, as the angel, that nothing is "too hard for the Lord" (Genesis 18:14).

My upcoming lesson was one of the first things I thought of when I got to the hospital. I realized my heart and mind had been prepared. I pondered about doing all that the Lord might ask of me. Could I also be like Abraham, as I climbed my mountain, and say with absolute faith, "Thy will be done," even if it required giving up Lexi? I cried out silently to God, "I know you were preparing me, but I don't want to be prepared. I cannot do this." I knew that God had done all he could to fortify me, but I didn't believe I was strong enough for the enormity of this trial.

As the hours went by, I continued to think about Abraham. I thought about how Isaac had been spared. Would my daughter be saved? Would there be a ram in the thicket for me? Part of me thought that she might be shielded and that the Lord was reminding me that He could do all things, as He did for Abraham. The other part of me thought that because I knew the ending to the story, there would be no need for faith on my behalf if she were shown mercy too. I would need to be obedient as Abraham and not expect her to live.

Never before in my life have I hungered and thirsted to "be filled with the Holy Ghost" (Luke 1:41) so that I could know the mind and will of the Lord. I desperately wanted to know what to ask for and what to receive through personal revelation. I yearned and sought diligently for that truth to enlighten and empower my mind. I didn't want to ask amiss. I knew trials were part of mortality, but so was God's love and mercy. The words I had read so often before came to my mind, "Yet will I not forget thee. Behold, I have graven thee upon the palms of my hands" (Isaiah 49:15–16).

I shared this story of Abraham, as well as my wrestle to know what to pray for, with my son JD. I confessed that maybe it wasn't God's will to spare Lexi. I wanted to make sure that as I prayed, I would only do what God would want.

After thinking about what I had said to him, JD had a flash of insight and came into the room. He looked at me in earnest. "Mom," he said, "I've been thinking about Abraham. I know that Abraham was willing to be obedient to the Lord even to the sacrificing of his son Isaac, but . . ."

Then he hesitated, trying to form his thoughts the way he had heard them in his mind so that there would be no misunderstanding. He calmly continued, "I think that Abraham probably pleaded with the Lord to show mercy on his son as he traveled to Mount Moriah." His eyes stared deeply into my own, hoping that I would understand what he was trying to say to me. It was a stunning revelation.

His words hit my heart, and I immediately knew that what he said was true. I said, "So you are saying that you believe that Abraham pleaded for God to change His will?" I shifted my weight, looking away from his gaze to ponder what he had just said to me and to let that concept sink in.

Pausing to collect my thoughts, I turned my eyes back to his. "You're right," I said. "In my studies of Abraham, the journey to Mount Moriah would have taken him three days . . . three *long* days."

There was a mutual understanding between JD and me of how truly excruciating those three days would have been for Abraham, now having gone through it ourselves. I continued thinking out loud, "He had three days to plead with the Lord to have mercy on him and his son."

I reached out and grabbed both of my son's hands and squeezed them before I wrapped my arms around him and hugged him, saying, "That is exactly what we are to do. You have given me the additional courage and faith and most importantly, the knowledge to go to the Lord and ask Him to change His plan for Lexi, as He did for Isaac." For it was "by faith Abraham, when he was tried, offered up Isaac . . . his only begotten son . . . Accounting that God was able to raise him up, even from the dead" (Hebrews 11:17, 19).

I was indecisive no longer. I knew like David that "in my distress I could call upon the Lord and I be delivered. f I asked not amiss. I turned my gaze back on Lexi and ever so lightly kissed her hand and laid my cheek on her arm. My love overflowed for her, for God, and for the knowledge that I might not have to let her go.

> *And the Lord said . . . I have prayed for thee, that thy faith fail not.*
>
> —Luke 22:31–32

Even if it had been God's intention to bring Lexi home to Him, we had the ability as a family and church and community to ask him to change those plans.

I was, nonetheless, hesitant to pray in that manner. But I realized that trusting God is also about immediately taking action on revelation given to us. Sometimes we trust and wait for God's will to unfold, but in this case, I knew that I wasn't just to accept His will—I was to ask for His will to be changed. How grateful I was that I was given these hours—which turned into days—to teach me to be bold in my prayers and to not allow my hope to falter.

During this time that I reflected on Abraham's experience,

my feelings for Abraham deepened, and I grew to love and understand him on a more personal level. What a tender mercy from the Lord that I had been preparing to teach the story of Abraham and Isaac the week I would be facing a similar trial. God had literally borne me on eagle's wings, as he did for the children of Israel, and brought me to Him (Exodus 19:4). Now fortified with understanding and power beyond my own, I knew that the Lord would answer my righteous desires if I would "seek him with [my] whole heart" (Psalm 119:2).

NOTE

1. George Q. Cannon, "Freedom of the Saints," in *Collected Discourses*, comp. Brian H. Stuy, 5 vols. [1987–92], 2:185.

Chapter Eight

THE MIRACLE OF MIGHTY PRAYER

But when they in their trouble did turn unto the Lord God of Israel, and sought him, he was found of them.

—2 Chronicles 15:4

The next morning, we learned that Lexi's chances of living were slimmer than we originally had supposed. When the paramedics had arrived at the scene of the accident, she'd had to be resuscitated, which meant she had some irreversible brain damage from the lack of oxygen entering her brain during the time between the accident and when resuscitation began. When she arrived at the hospital, she was assessed by doctors, who gave her no chance of survival. They weren't even going to take the time to stitch up her face, and the organ donation team had been contacted and were already at the hospital before we got there.

To show how severe Lexi's injury was, the doctor also explained to us that her initial GCS (Glasgow Coma Scale) score[1] when she arrived at the hospital was three, which is the lowest possible score (indicating a deep coma or death). The highest score, for a fully awake person, is fifteen. To reiterate how low Lexi's score really was, he pointed to a chair in the room and told us that the chair had the same functionality as someone with a GCS of a three. I gasped at the suggestion. I didn't know how to respond. His words bore down upon me.

I looked at Lexi. It was just too hard to believe that she had been as alive as a chair. The comparison made me think about how lively she had always been. I mean, this was Lexi, the girl who had just competed in a Tough Mudder race.

She had come home from that race caked in mud from head to toe, her body aching. After she had plunged into frigid water filled with ice chunks, hypothermia had set in, but she stubbornly refused to quit. She was unconquerable; she was the only girl that day (that she knew of) to scale a skateboarding ramp. With clenched teeth, she sprinted up the side as she miraculously caught her friend's hand, making it to the top. Her face flushed, gasping for air, she relished the challenge, not the slightest trace of fear in her body. The memory lifted some of the sorrow, but only for an instant.

The Lord thy God, he it is that doth go with thee; he will not fail thee, nor forsake thee.
—Deuteronomy 31:6

The doctors continued to emphasize that despite the fact that she had made it through the night, she still did not have much of a chance of survival. She already had swelling in her brain, and this swelling would continue to get worse. It was just a matter of time to know how destructive the swelling would be.[2]

And because her injury was in the lower, central part of her brain, there was not much they could do to combat the swelling. In more external brain injuries, the top of the skull can be removed to relieve the pressure on the brain, but this was not the case with Lexi. We knew of others that had suffered similar injuries who had died within a few days because of swelling in the brain.

We were told we had a long road ahead of us. After an initial injury to the brain, it can take up to two weeks to reach its maximum point of swelling. So, the doctors indicated that it would be seven to ten days before they would know for sure if she would make it. There was never any doubt in my mind of God's miraculous power, but would it be His will to have her stay?

It was easy to pull back into my sanctuary of memories to help calm my troubled heart. Throughout the years, Lexi loved to make mischief and play pranks. For example, one morning, she awoke early to catch some ducks in a pond near our house. She chased and darted through the park after her feathered friends, but with no success. Until one wild moment, she gave it a final attempt, diving over a bush, arms outstretched, miraculously catching a straggler. Laughing and giggling, she caught her breath before putting the duck inside a box and into the trunk of her car.

Arriving at her high school, she discreetly let the duck out of its confinement and swooshed it inside the building to roam the halls, all while beaming from ear to ear that she had actually accomplished her mission. She had gone to all that trouble just to see the students' reactions. She could be who she was and was not afraid of what others might think. She liked to be different.

I paused long enough in my thoughts for a fleeting smile. Sitting by Lexi's bed, I tenderly planted a kiss on her arm. Daylight had vanished. It felt like two weeks had passed, and I had to remind myself that the accident happened only the night before. I was utterly exhausted, both physically and spiritually. When my daughter Kelsi came in the room, I mentioned how time seemed to stand still to her. Seconds later, my son Parker walked in the room and put forth the very same sentiment.

Knowing how the events of the past twenty-four hours had taken a toll on my body, my family insisted that I go to the family guesthouse³ across the street from the hospital to get some sleep that night. Even though I didn't want to leave Lexi, I agreed to go, if only for a few hours. I didn't understand why the Lord would not see fit in His infinite wisdom to give His peace to me to disperse "the thick darkness" (1 Kings 8:12) from me. Yet I would still continue to knock on heaven's door, waiting impatiently to be invited in.

> *I am weary with my groaning; all the night make I my bed to swim; I water my couch with my tears.*
>
> —Psalm 6:6

"I am weary with my groaning" (Psalm 6:6), I cried

out in the darkness. "Evening, and morning, and at noon" (Psalm 55:17), I prayed aloud for God to hear me. My soul hungered for his "marvellous light" (1 Peter 2:9), so I knelt and cried mightily unto God. I had prayed all day, and at night I continued to pray, hoping my petitions would reach the heavens.

I wanted to lay my burden at the Lord's feet for Him to take it away. I cried out to the Lord for deliverance, to escape the harrowing torment I was in. I explained to Him that there were many people praying for me to receive peace. And I reminded Him of others that had received peace—even when they had lost loved ones.

But I continued to battle the blackness, feeling that if I did not receive solace soon, my heart would break under the weight of my grief. This was the most ominous moment of my life, and I needed the darkness banished from my soul. The silence of the heavens was deafening. Had not Christ said, "Come unto me, all ye that . . . are heavy laden, and I will give you rest" (Matthew 11:28)? Why couldn't I receive this rest for my spirit? Why couldn't peace prevail? I lay awake the entire night and did not cease to pray, yet the pain continued even as I was persistent in my pleadings for healing.

As I continued to feel such intense agony of spirit, I became acquainted with God in a more intimate way. It was as if I had to go through my own Gethsemane to understand in a small way what the Savior endured for all of us. I gained a greater depth of appreciation for the Savior's words, "I have trodden the winepress alone" (Isaiah 63:3). I knew that He had been there with me all along, but I felt completely and utterly alone. The agony that threatened to wash over me and sink me in despair would not dissipate and seemed to stretch to eternity.

During the night, I continued to remember Abraham.

Knowing that it wasn't a coincidence that I had prepared to teach the lesson of Abraham and Isaac on the week of Lexi's accident should have made it much easier for me to believe that Lexi would be saved. Yet I found myself like the woman with the issue of blood, hiding timidly in a crowded market place, wondering if someone as ordinary as myself could be worthy of asking for such a healing. Abraham was a prophet and I was . . . well, I felt ordinary—not important enough to receive such a miracle.

However, as I thought of the story of the woman, I realized that by her actions, she was actually the only courageous person in the crowd. She believed with all her heart that if she could just touch the hem of the Savior's garment, she would be healed. She didn't wait for Him to stop and acknowledge her or for Him to put His hands on her head to bless her. She just knew instinctively that His very being was so filled with power and glory that by touching His clothing, she would be made whole. I wondered if I was putting a limit on His gift to us. I found out that as soon as I could touch the Savior and feel His love, I too was healed (see Mark 5:25–34).

I hurried across the street to the hospital around four in the morning. I had only slept a couple hours, so I thought I might as well go back. I had prayed all night, but I continued to pray into the morning by Lexi's bedside.

A couple hours later, the whole room was bathed in a warm glow as the early morning sunlight broke over the mountain and peeked through the windows. A warm sensation sent a wave of peace through my soul. It engulfed me, soothed my heart, and dissolved the pain. My aching wounds were replaced with joy and happiness as if the sun itself had chased away my darkness.

The light flooded into my heart, and a burst of warmth pressed into my chest. But it was His Son that brought this change. It was His peace that engulfed my soul. My heart was open to an understanding that a ram had been found. "The Holy Ghost [taught me] in that same hour" (Luke 12:12) with such clarity—I knew that Lexi would be healed.

I felt to cry as Jeremiah, "I [was] pained at my very heart; my heart maketh a noise in me" (Jeremiah 4:19), yet now I could "rejoice with joy unspeakable" (1 Peter 1:8) as my "sorrow [was] turned into joy" (John 16:20). Without warning, a single tear broke on my lap. Tilting my head back, I looked heavenward and whispered a reverent, "Thank you."

> *How excellent is thy lovingkindness, O God! Therefore the children of men put their trust under the shadow of they wings. . . . In thy light shall we see light.*
>
> —Psalm 36:7, 9

My voice quivered with emotion, pools of tears now clouding my vision. "I can't believe that you are letting her stay," I whispered in wonder and awe. The Spirit filled me. My emotions were caught in my throat; I didn't want to breathe. Tears streaked my cheeks but I didn't brush them away. Any movement I feared might allow the Spirit to flee. I wanted to capture this moment, to bask in its warmth. Could heaven be any closer than this?

A newfound power surged through me like an unquenchable fire burning in my breast. I stole a quick glance at Lexi. Then watching her intently, a twinge of excitement filled me, knowing that soon I'd see her smile, feel the kindness in her eyes, and hear her infectious laugh. I was overwhelmed with gratitude—I had not been forgotten. I dropped to my knees; a sob of joy tore from my soul.

When Jesus told His disciples that His friend Lazarus had

died, He made an interesting statement: "And I am glad for your sakes that I was not there, to the intent ye may believe" (John 11:15). Was this the same lesson He was teaching me and that He teaches all of us when He allows us to suffer for a while so we might come to a greater understanding of belief and experience? When belief turns into knowledge? The eternal gratitude I felt for Christ's suffering was now magnified. I had a personal reassurance that God was near; He spoke to my heart, "I have heard thy prayer, I have seen thy tears: behold, I will heal thee" (2 Kings 20:5). The accompanying strength and courage received from the positive assurance that Lexi would be healed brought rejoicing, and my spirit soared.

Like David, who wrote in Psalm 40:1, "I waited patiently for the Lord; and he inclined unto me, and heard my cry." What a miraculous healing for my spirit! I had received a witness after "the trial of [my] faith" (1 Peter 1:7). I was changed. I was no longer alone.

God truly "is able to succour them that are [hurting]"

> When through the deep waters I call thee to go,
> The rivers of sorrow shall not thee o'erflow,
> For I will be with thee thy troubles to bless,
> And sanctify to thee thy deepest distress.
>
> The soul that on Jesus hath leaned for repose,
> I will not, I cannot, deseret to his foes,
> That soul, though all hell should endeavor to shake,
> I'll never, no never, no never forsake.
>
> —"How Firm a Foundation"[4]

(Hebrews 2:18). I had learned years earlier that *succor* means to "run to," which helped me visualize the Savior running to my side in my hour of need, personalizing this scripture in a tender way.

What a remarkable gift to *know*, even before she came out of her coma, that Lexi would stay with us and be whole and well again. I am grateful that the Lord loved me enough to stretch my soul and say in effect, "Call unto me, and I will answer thee, and shew thee great and mighty things, which thou knowest not" (Jeremiah 33:3).

NOTES

1. A GCS (Glasgow Coma Scale) score is used to evaluate how conscious and responsive someone is after a traumatic brain injury and to help gauge the severity of the injury.

2. Brain swelling "can quickly cause serious problems—including death. It's also usually more difficult to treat. . . . The thick, bony skull that snugly protects this vital organ provides little room for the brain to swell" ("Brain Swelling," *WebMD*, last updated September 11, 2016, https://www.webmd.com/brain/brain-swelling-brain-edema-intracranial-pressure#1.

3. The guest house is a place the hospital offers, at a minimal price, for families whose loved ones are in critical care in order to be close to them.

4. "How Firm a Foundation," *Hymns*, no. 85.

Chapter Nine

THE MIRACLE
OF CHARITY

*And we have known and believed the love that God hath
to us. God is love; and he that dwelleth in love dwelleth in
God, and God in him.*

—1 John 4:16

If the ten-and-a-half-hour van ride didn't bond our family, the beach was sure to do it. A gentle sea breeze brushed through my hair as the kids scampered out of the van to the sun-drenched beach, sand squishing between their toes. With a family of eleven on a tight budget, going out to eat and paying for plane tickets were out of the question. But the kids didn't seem to notice as they bodysurfed through waves and flew kites on the overcast day.

Plastic buckets swinging by their side, they collected seashells that had gently washed ashore as the kids soaked up the sun. They cheered when sandcastles were left erect from crushing

waves and giggled when some became engulfed and washed mysteriously away.

"If only our summers were endless," I mused. It was here that we found a place separating us from the rest of the world. It drew us back year after year. The kids were best friends and relished the time spent together. They were fiercely loyal to one another and learned to forgive easily. Many times, people observing our family commented on how impressed they were that our children seemed to genuinely love each other and want to be together.

So it was a great joy when my children who lived out of state and their families finally began arriving Thursday morning, the day after Lexi's accident, to be together again. They had come with heavy and broken hearts, thinking they were returning to Utah to attend a funeral. Shelby and her husband, Brandon, arrived first with their boys; and then shortly after, Cassidy and Daniel came with their son, Calvin. JD and his wife, McCall, and their girls were last to arrive after a fifteen-hour flight delay. When I looked up to see JD walking toward me, we fought back tears as we hugged each other in a warm embrace. It had been a long day for both of us.

Although we were filled with sadness, it was wonderful to be together again. We hugged, wept, and received strength from one another. Sharing our pain together seemed to lessen it. They gave me strength when I felt my soul was empty.

My children from out of state had been going through their own set of emotions. It was horrible for them to be so far away, to be without the support of the family. Lexi's sister Cassidy told me how the night had seemed endless, filled with tears and more tears. She hated that she was not able to rush to the hospital that night, but had to wait until morning to leave, enduring a three-hour, grueling plane ride with no communication. It was torture.

73

During the flight, she sobbed and prayed and prayed and sobbed. At times, she felt that Lexi would be all right, but doubts would soon sneak in, and she feared Lexi would not make it.

> The God of my rock; in him will I trust: he is my shield, and the horn of my salvation, my high tower, and my refuge, my savior."
>
> —2 Samuel 22:3

Seventeen hours after Cassidy got the fateful call, she walked into Lexi's room. Her heart dropped. This was not Lexi. She seemed lifeless, very close to slipping away. Cassidy wanted so badly for Lexi to wake up—to see her smile again. The thought that Lexi might not ever talk to her again started to sneak into her mind, and the tears returned with a vengeance. "Be strong for your family; they need you," she kept repeating to herself.

She walked to Lexi's side and touched her as if to wake her from sleep. "Lexi, it's me. Lexi, don't leave. Lexi, we need you," Cassidy pleaded. She felt like it was a dream. But despite all the terror she experienced up to that point, she also felt a peace in the room, an immense power from on high.

Witnessing this, I was reminded that my family was changing. With Lexi's accident, I knew that things would never be the same. The first time I had that feeling in my heart was ten years earlier. I had struggled to say goodbye to my oldest son, McKay, who was going off to college just thirty minutes away. Standing on our front porch, the entire family gathered and waved goodbye, tears welling up in our eyes. I tried to be strong and smother the thought, but I couldn't hold back the tears as my son pulled away from the house in his red beat-up car, his belongings spilling from boxes piled high on the seats.

All of a sudden, he slammed on his brakes, pulled himself

through the driver's side window and smiled broadly and while pounding his fist in the air and shouted, "Hurrah for Israel! Hurrah for Israel! Hurrah for Israel!"

Instantly the mood changed. Tears were forgotten as cheers erupted. "Hurrah for Israel, Hurrah for Israel!" we shouted back, grinning wildly. The exuberance was catching, and as his car drove off, we sprinted from the porch, chasing him down the street, cheering wildly and as loudly as we could, hoping that he would hear us as we continued to chant, "Hurrah, hurrah for Israel." The splatter of bare feet against the pavement persisted until he turned a corner and the car was a distant memory.

McKay knew instinctively that this cheer would lift the spirits of his siblings. But it did more than boost our spirits; there was an unspoken message that no matter what happened to us when we were apart, we would remain faithful and true to God, even during the hard times. If it had been appropriate in the hospital, that cheer would have erupted again. We would be steadfast, even if we were to lose our Lexi—our daughter, our sister, our friend.

As we gathered in Lexi's room, one of the first things we each thought about was what our last conversation had been with her. While we were discussing these last interactions, we found that all of us had made contact with her sometime in the last week and that everyone had ended their conversation by telling Lexi that they loved her. We felt a sense of relief as we realized that we had prioritized staying in contact with each other. There was no tinge of regret.

The kids don't always communicate with each other weekly, but it was a tender mercy from God that He had prompted each of them to contact Lexi in some way that week. It seemed to lift our burden just a little, knowing that we had recently reached out to her and expressed love. An even greater feeling of relief came as we realized that not one person had said an unkind word to her in recent memory. There were no regrets and no feelings of guilt. I realized I wouldn't have even been able to breathe if there had even been a sharp tone in my recent words to Lexi. Our family is not perfect, but with the circumstances, we were grateful to see that we had done things right.

> But the fruit of the Spirit is love.
> —Galatians 5:22

Lexi made it easy for the family to express their love openly because whenever any of her siblings left our house after coming over for dinner or for a visit, Lexi would rush to the door, give them a hug, and tell them that she loved them. Those individuals that had just married into the family were surprised by her spontaneous and childlike expression. But as soon as they joined the family, there was never a visit that she didn't utter the words "I love you" to them as well.

> Above all these things put on charity.
> —Colossians 3:14

It is a goal for my family to not let disputes, contentious

feelings, or disagreements carry on day after day. As the scriptures teach, "Let there be no strife, I pray thee, between me and thee . . . for we be brethren" (Genesis 13:8).

When my children were young, instead of sending them to time out when they said or did something unkind to their siblings, I had them go to their rooms and write a note about something good they saw in the sibling they had quarreled with. It was gratifying to see how quickly their hearts would change and how a feeling of love would reenter our home by that simple act to strengthen each other "in all holy conversation" (2 Peter 3:11).

The days in the hospital continued to pass slowly as we waited for Lexi to come out of her coma, but now we were together, and that made all the difference. Each day we would kneel together in family prayer, thanking God for the small miracles we would see throughout the day. When we were blessed to have our entire family allowed in Lexi's room, we experienced a tiny slice of heaven as we knelt down in a circle around her bed holding hands. The Spirit was always so intense that we felt we were getting a small glimpse of what Zion would be like. We continued to bear one another's burdens. A familiar feeling of heaven no longer seemed out of reach. I didn't want the warmth and the unique strength of these quiet, sacred moments to dissolve.

Sometimes, as I sat next to Lexi's hospital bed, memories of my own parents would come to my mind. I took the time to ponder. I had been blessed to be born of God-fearing parents. The principles they espoused shaped my life. They were rooted deeply in my soul from a young age. I felt joy as I remembered specific experiences.

It was still dark outside when I was awakened by music blasting through the house. Within minutes, my door swung open, and the light turned on. Squinting and trying to adjust my eyes, I saw my dad standing in the doorway smiling broadly as he sang, "Top of the morning, it's a bright and sunny day, eggs over easy just to chase your cares away."

How I wanted to sink back down into my cozy pillow and get a few more winks before I had to go to school, but the music was too loud. And I could hear my mom bustling around in the kitchen getting breakfast ready. If it weren't for the smell of waffles and bacon and the cheeriness of my dad's voice, it would have been a challenge to get up in the wee morning hours for our regular family scripture study before the sun dared show its face.

My parents knew that without anchoring our souls in God, we would be unprepared for the Lord's coming, like the foolish virgins who, "while the bridegroom tarried . . . all slumbered and slept" (Matthew 25:5). They were like Nehemiah in the Old Testament, who said, "I am doing a great work, so that I cannot come down: why should the work cease, whilst I leave it, and come down to you?" (Nehemiah 6:3)

These early mornings and the Monday nights, where we

prayed, sang, and learned about the Savior together, rooted my mind and heart so deeply to God and taught me that He would not forsake me. Those times shaped my life.

It was my parent's example that helped me raise my children with that same level of commitment, where nothing—sports, activities, or friends—would come before God's teachings. Every Sunday and every single morning would be devoted to learning from the scriptures and trying to become more like God. No exceptions. Therefore, the scriptures became a protective shield from the threatening war of the world surrounding the hearts of my family.

My mind came back to the room in the hospital, enveloped in the company of my family. As we sat in the same room, I looked lovingly at each person, and my heart felt full to overflowing.

> Call unto me, and I will answer thee, and shew thee great and mighty things, which thou knowest not.
>
> —Jeremiah 33:3

Being with Lexi was drawing us together in a deeper bond as we clung to one another. We noticed we were developing more love for each other.

The hours and days wore on. I remember one afternoon sitting with my daughter-in-law McCall by Lexi's bed. Neither of us were talking—because her room needed to be quiet in order for her brain to heal—but both of us understood each other's pain. As I sat in that spiritual place, I felt my love grow stronger for Lexi and McCall. This love increased the same way with each member of my family as we spent hour after hour in Lexi's room. How blessed we were to have a greater outpouring of love come into our hearts for each other. Lexi's room became a holy temple to us.

My daughter Cassidy explains our feelings perfectly:

> The thing I will always remember about this whole experience is the immense love that embraced my family. The moment I arrived at the hospital, I felt love, a pure love, for each one of my family members. As we gathered for many family prayers, I felt love. I felt love as we sat quietly in Lexi's room. For those few days, it was as if time stood still and nothing else in the world mattered. And nothing did except for my family and my knowledge of the gospel. The love we had for each other was magnified deeply, and it continued to grow with each passing day. There were no quarrels or disputations among us, only love, kindness, gratitude, and selflessness toward one another. For me, it felt as if we were living in a piece of heaven. We were all striving for goodness so our Lexi would be healed.

The bond of love and the faith we shared strengthened us and carried us through the difficult time. Through our faith, we were able to cast fears aside and strive for a perfect love. Just as John declared, "There is no fear in love; but perfect love casteth out fear" (1 John 4:18). Although we don't always understand the Lord's purpose, recognizing His deep love for us assures us that we can always trust in Him.

As Nancy Murphy, a professor of Christian philosophy, explains in her book *Whisperings of the Spirit*, "During the difficult times of our lives, we can imagine the Lord asking, 'Do you know why this is happening to you?' With complete faith in his infinite wisdom and his eternal perspective, we can then say to him, 'No, but you do.'"[1]

Cassidy continued:

> The Lord knows all things, and in His wisdom, He knows what will bring about the most rapid spiritual growth in our lives, moving us as quickly as possible along the path to perfection. This accelerated spiritual progression many times comes as a result of our trials. Despite difficulty and pain, it is in this way that challenges can greatly bless our lives.
>
> Our family has been a witness of this truth, and I know as we strive to love and trust in the Lord, we will be able to endure all things. When we cast away our fears and love perfectly, all things will become brighter, and we will see how the Lord sees us and our fellow men. May we all strive to embrace each other with a perfect love.

The perfect love Cassidy describes is called charity in the scriptures: "Charity suffereth long, and is kind; charity envieth not; charity vaunteth not itself, is not puffed up, doth not behave itself unseemly, seeketh not her own, is not easily provoked, thinketh no evil; rejoiceth not in iniquity, but rejoiceth in the truth; beareth all things, believeth all things, hopeth all things, endureth all things. . . . And now abideth faith, hope, charity, these three; but the greatest of these is charity" (1 Corinthians 13:4–7, 13).

NOTE

1. Nancy Murphy, *Whisperings of the Spirit* (Salt Lake City: Deseret Book, 2012), 51.

Chapter Ten

THE MIRACLE TO KNOW THE HEAVENS ARE NOT SILENT

Rabbi, we know that thou art a teacher come from God: for no man can do these miracles that thou doest, except God be with him.

—John 3:2

My son Parker is only a year younger than Lexi. It was hard for them to be at the tail end of the family. It seemed like overnight five of their older siblings, who had been living at home, went off to college or got married (two had left two years before). It was just the two of them at home when Lexi started high school—a family of nine children down to two in a few years. Being at the end of our big family, they had always been close, and they considered each other best friends. Lexi was the perfect older sister, watching out for Parker's every need. If his friends were busy on a Saturday night, she had him tag along with her—even if she had a date. He was the one she would confide in about boys, and he would tell her his secret crushes. He was her sidekick—the one she would call to go with her on her spontaneous adventures.

On one of their favorite outings, they rounded a bend along the river bank ducking to miss the low overhanging branches that lined the river enclosing their secluded hideout. The forest of trees wrapped around the edge of the bank making it almost impossible to discover, forming a canopy of sorts to hide their secret. It was Lexi's favorite place to go. It beckoned to her of freedom. And the cluster of trees provided needed shade on a warm, muggy day.

As they entered the clearing, Lexi could hardly contain her excitement. Pushing off with her right foot, she launched from the bridge, gliding effortlessly through the air and then striking the water. Her eyes showed no fear. Floating in the river, she drifted a few yards, fending off some low-level branches until she found a large, sturdy branch with which to pull herself out to the far bank.

The current was not strong enough to sweep her farther down, but the icy cold water forced her to retreat. A few feeble rays of sun slipped through the trees, pouring much-needed heat through her entire body. She felt freer than a bird suddenly released from its cage.

Parker followed suit, sail-ing through the air, knees tucked tight under his chin, hitting the water with a mighty

As they entered the clear-ing, Lexi could hardly con-tain her excitement. Pushing off with her right foot, she launched from the bridge,

gliding effortlessly through the air and then splash. Parker waded out up onto the rocks, drops of water lingering on his skin, as he playfully shook his dripping hair, spraying Lexi.

Goosebumps spread over her arms and legs as the wind rus-tled through the aspens. She pulled her knees close to her chest and wrapped her arms snugly around them for warmth as they had forgotten their towels. This was the life. Parker knew his world could never be dull when Lexi was with him. The twinkle in her eyes was forever present.

The possibility of them being separated during this earth life was too much for him to handle. For the first couple of nights in the hospital, Parker was devastated at the thought of losing his sister and best friend. He thought many times, *I can't lose Lexi! I don't know what I'd do without her. You can't do this to me, Heavenly Father!*

After two days of turmoil, he was desperate for peace and willing to accept whatever the Lord had in store for his sister. He went home from the hospital that evening and prayed to Heavenly Father for peace. After he prayed, he felt inspired to open up his scriptures. As he did, they fell open to Acts 9:36–41, and these are the words he read:

> Now there was at Joppa a certain disciple named Tabitha . . . this woman was full of good works and almsdeeds which she did.
>
> And it came to pass in those days, that she was sick, and died: whom when they had washed, they laid her in an upper chamber.
>
> . . . The disciples had heard that Peter was there, they sent unto him two men, desiring him that would not delay to come to them.
>
> Then Peter arose and went with them. When he was come, they brought him into the upper chamber: and all the widows stood by him weeping. . . .
>
> But Peter put them all forth, and keeled down, and prayed; and turning him to the body said, Tabitha, arise. And she opened her eyes: and when she saw Peter, she sat up.
>
> And he gave her his hand, and lifted her up, and when he had called the saints and widows, presented her alive.

As Parker read these verses, written long ago by an ancient prophet, he felt an overpowering sense of comfort and knew that Lexi would be all right. He realized that like Tabitha, Lexi was also full of good works and was worthy of a miracle. He had read these words before but had just skimmed them, for he had witnessed many great miracles in our day. He knew it was not an accident that he read this story at this exact time when Lexi was in need of such a miracle. He felt God was reminding him that He could and would continue to perform miracles. Now these same words pierced his heart and spoke comfort to him. He knew they were true! Of course God was still a God of miracles. He loves all His children the same whether they be born in this century or during Christ's lifetime. He would "have faith and doubt not" knowing that "whatsoever [he should] ask in prayer, believing, [he would] receive" (Matthew 21:21, 22).

Tears welled up in his eyes—his mourning changed to joy for the first time since the accident. He knew this was a direct answer from the Lord because of the fervent prayers he had offered on Lexi's behalf. In the scriptures, he had found comfort from the Prince of Peace. He knelt down and thanked Heavenly Father for showing him those exact verses. Hope was now his companion as his soul expanded with faith.

Early the next morning, Parker couldn't wait to return to the hospital. With an air of calm, he went to the ICU where he found me seated, as usual, beside Lexi's bed and pulled up a chair. He had his scriptures with him and opened to the exact spot he had read the night before. His voice trembled slightly with emotion as he whispered, "Mom, I know Lexi will be okay."

Believe ye that I am able to do this? They said unto him, Yea, Lord. Then touched he their eyes, saying, According to your faith be it unto you.

—Matthew 9:28–29

I looked at him quizzically, waiting for him to finish. He

pushed the scriptures toward me, his voice lowered even more, and he began to tell me of his experience the night before.

After I read the passage for myself, we both looked at each other and smiled as tears trickled down our faces. I was astonished at how explicit his answer was, leaving no room for confusion or doubt. What a testimony to Parker that God knew him and knew of his love for his sister. God chose to send a direct message to him that Lexi would live.

Parker's faith and diligence in listening to the Spirit was another witness for me and my family that Lexi would be made whole. As we pondered this gift our Heavenly Father had given to him, our faith was unshaken in the knowledge that God's hand was in every detail of this miracle. It was true that if we put our "trust in the Lord: he [would be our] help and [our] shield," for he was "mindful of us: he [would] bless us" (Psalm 115:11–12). We knew for ourselves that it was God who would make Lexi whole again. It was amazing to see how Parker's demeanor had changed. He was happy again. There was no room for fear.

I needed these constant reminders from my family that it *was* God's will that Lexi be made whole. Because the prognosis given by each doctor was grim, we knew her healing would be nothing short of a miracle. Parker's words continued to keep me in a good place, especially as Lexi continued to struggle. That passage of scripture would forever burn within.

> Blessed is the man that trusteth in the Lord, and whose hope the Lord is.
>
> —Jeremiah 17:7

Shortly after Parker shared his experience with me, JD joined us in the room and remarked, "Even lying on this hospital bed in a coma, she is stunning." The other family members in the room agreed, nodding thoughtfully. One of them said, "That's just what I have been thinking."

I glanced over at Lexi, and I, too, was astonished at her uncommon beauty. She was pretty but unpretentious. At five feet seven inches, she had a slim frame and flawless olive skin, which deepened due to endless hours of tennis and outside labor. But her arms and hands were still smooth and delicate.

I had always been amazed at her work ethic. On a typical Saturday morning in our house, no one slept in, even though all my kids were teenagers now. I would hear footsteps below my room around 6:30 a.m., the kids in the kitchen getting their breakfast before hitching up the trailer with the lawn mower to take off for their landscaping business.

Saturday was Lexi's busiest day. She mowed, edged, and weeded until 11 a.m. and then got a quick bite before taking off to practice tennis. After tennis, she would have a few hours to study before changing her clothes to work at a nearby restaurant. She worked tirelessly for her money and saved almost every penny to pay for college and her mission.

Returning my attention to our conversation in Lexi's hospital room, I said, "You know, there are two things I miss most about Lexi. One is seeing her blue eyes. They are so full of life."

Then turning to look at JD, I asked, "Didn't you feel that

through her eyes you could see her trusting heart?" He nodded in agreement.

Then, cocking my head to my left to look at Parker, I continued, "And what do you think is the second attribute that I have yearned to see again?" In unison both my boys said confidently, "Her smile."

"Yup. It is electrifying," I said. It was easy to see they concurred with my assessment.

"And now all of us know for ourselves that the heavens aren't silent. It's just a matter of time until we see her smile again. God has spoken to each of us, and His words couldn't have been clearer than those he spoke to Parker when he directed him to that passage of scripture in Acts. God has been so good and kind to our family. The Lord is mindful of every detail."

My daughter Shelby wrote the following about receiving personal revelation in the hospital:

> The most profound lesson I learned through this was how important personal revelation is. I was reminded that the Lord answers prayer. I learned the importance of trusting the Lord. Before Lexi's accident, I always prayed but didn't have the faith that I do now that He would help me. Now I can't go a day without asking for guidance or help for a specific challenge. It's crazy that I never used this power to the extent that I could have. We all have trials. Some come in the form of finances, marriage, children, or in ways we don't usually think about—like feelings of loneliness or unfulfilled hopes and dreams. Moreover, with every challenge, the Lord pleads that we will come to Him in prayer. The Lord is there; He will give us personal revelation and answer our prayers. Whether your challenges or questions are big or small, He cares.

Chapter Eleven

THE MIRACLE OF STANDING FIRMLY IN FAITH

And he said, The Lord is my rock, and my fortress, and my deliverer; The God of my rock; in him will I trust: he is my shield, and the horn of my salvation, my high tower, and my refuge, my saviour; thou savest me from violence.

—2 Samuel 22:2–3

I had been given the knowledge through the Holy Ghost that Lexi would be healed and go on to live a normal life. This assurance came through private and family prayers, coupled with prayers by the laying on of hands and personal revelation.

All of the prayers that Lexi received were powerful and direct, testifying that she would be healed. Yet it was easy to fall from that level of faith whenever a doctor or therapist came to check on her, as they would always repeat the same prognosis that Lexi's chances of making it were slim. They would remind me that for the next five to seven days the probability of losing Lexi was still very high, and that even if she did survive, she'd most likely end up in a care center for the rest of her life because of the shearing that had occurred in her brain.

As they were the experts, I'd allow doubts to creep back into my mind and create a distance from God's promise to me. Their words forced a battle to rage between my mind and my heart, which would chip away at my faith. Yet I knew that "with God all things are possible" (Matthew 19:26) if I could just "ask in faith, nothing wavering." (James 1:6). I couldn't allow the doctors' bleak, but honest, evaluations stop me from having the faith to move mountains. I'd been taught that faith *is* another word for power.

There was one therapist whom I remember particularly for his cheerful countenance. He was positive and happy and told me not to worry. He had seen many patients recover who had been hit by cars as long as they hit the windshield and not the

And it was "by faith Enoch was translated that he should not see death." It was "by faith Noah, being warned of God of things not seen as yet . . . prepared an ark to the saving of his house." Again, it was "by faith Moses . . . passed through the Red sea as by dry land: which the Egyptians assaying to do were drowned." And finally, it was "by faith the walls of Jericho fell down, after they were compassed about seven days."

—Hebrews 11:5, 7, 23, 29–30

metal bar above the windshield. For those people who hit the bar, there was no hope because the bar does not give.

I flinched at his words and my faith faltered. Interrupting, I told him that the bar was exactly where Lexi's head had hit the car. His countenance changed abruptly, and an uncomfortable silence filled the air.

His eyes dropped to look down at his feet, and refusing to look me in the eye, he managed to mutter, "I'm sorry," before looking away. Again, my faith dipped a little.

I only needed to look to the book of Hebrews for my direction. "Cast not away therefore your confidence, which hath great recompence of reward. For ye have need of patience, that, after ye have done the will of God, ye might receive the promise" (Hebrews 10:35–36).

The scriptures were full of examples for me to follow. It was only *after* David had faith that he could go face the giant Goliath. I, too, had to have this faith *before* the miracle could happen. I needed to keep these scripture stories foremost in my mind. Faith was the key. Yet sometimes, I felt the weight of my fear becoming so heavy I could not feel the lightness the Spirit brings. Why couldn't I be like Enoch, whose faith was so great that "he spake the word of the Lord, and the earth trembled, and the mountains fled" (Moses 7:13)? My courage could not falter. I could "be not afraid of their faces" (Jeremiah 1:8) for it was God that said "I have made thee this day a defenced city, and an iron pillar . . . against the people of the land. And they shall fight against thee; but they shall not prevail against thee; for I am with thee . . . to deliver thee" (Jeremiah 1:18–19).

On the afternoon of the second day after the accident, I realized what my problem was. In the New Testament, there is a beautiful passage describing how the Savior walks on the sea toward His disciples who are in a ship. When Peter asks the Savior if he can walk out to Him, the Lord invites him to come. And when Peter's eyes are focused on the Savior, he is able to walk on the water, but when he looks away from the Savior, the waves become daunting, and he sinks.

> Be still my soul: Thy God doth undertake,
> To guide the future as he has the past.
> Thy hope, thy confidence let nothing shake.
> All now mysterious shall be bright at last.
> Be still, my soul: The waves and winds still know
> His voice who ruled them while he dwelt below.
>
> —"Be Still, My Soul"[1]

I had kept my eyes focused on the Savior, but, like Peter, when I saw the rough waves and strong, boisterous winds come, I stopped looking toward Christ and would begin to sink. I felt to cry out as did Peter, "Lord, save me" (Matthew 14:30). Could I rid myself of this fear and continue to be fixed on heaven's purpose and reach up to grasp the Savior's outstretched hand? For I knew that "God hath not given us the spirit of fear; but of power, and of love, and of a sound mind" (2 Timothy 1:7).

Fear was my stumbling block. I needed to be reminded of the Lord's limitless power and to turn to Him with full purpose of heart, "for with God nothing [is] impossible" (Luke 1:37). I decided I needed to have a visual image of the Savior in my mind the next time a doctor came into the room.

A few minutes after making this plan, I was tested. A doctor came in to explain, yet again, what the outcome for Lexi was probably going to be. I began to challenge myself by fastening my eyes only on the Savior. Although the doctor thought I was looking at him, my eyes were instead fixed on an image in my mind of the Savior next to him. I could feel the Savior's gaze upon me and hear His words telling me to be of good cheer. As I saw Christ in my mind's eye, my soul was immediately filled with the fire of faith. When the doctor was finished talking, I realized my faith was still intact. I had pushed back against the weakness that had threatened my resolve, and I had not let the doctor's words wash over me and sink me into despair. Shortly after the doctor left, my daughter Cassidy came into the room, and I excitedly told her, "I didn't sink! I didn't sink!" I hugged her, and she rejoiced with me in my feat. I had asked, believing that I'd receive, and it was given me (see Matthew 21:22; 7:7).

I had learned an important lesson of choosing faith and hope instead of fear. From that point on, that was how I made it through each of the doctors' visits. I was filled with hope. For me, the doctors' words were as daunting as the storm Peter faced, but our Savior has said, "Therefore walk with me" (Moses 6:34), and that is what I learned to do. Do we accept God's offer to walk with Him by standing firmly in faith? In Acts 16:23, it says Paul and Silas were beaten and then cast into prison. Their life seemed bleak indeed. Yet in verse 25, it says, "And at midnight Paul and Silas prayed, and sang praises unto God." They chose to walk with God in faith, joy, and thanksgiving.

I also learned through this experience that when I did sink, the Savior's hand was outstretched, ready to lift me back up to His side, just as he did for Peter: "And *immediately* Jesus stretched forth his hand, and caught him" (Matthew 14:31; italics added).

The hand of Christ had already come to me in many different ways. It came to me when Tanner bore his testimony to me, when

Parker told me of his sacred experience that God was still a God of miracles, and when JD shared several scripture stories with me. I realized that each time I had struggled to maintain the level of faith needed for a miracle, His hand was always there, waiting for me to reach out, grasp it, and hold on.

Each of my children had learned from Christ's example how to extend an outstretched hand. Just like Peter having learned the power that came from Christ's outstretched hand when he began to sink and was able to extend this same gift to others after Christ's resurrection. At the temple was a lame man asking alms. "Peter fastening his eyes upon him with John, said, Look on us . . . In the name of Jesus Christ of Nazareth rise up and walk. And he took him by the right hand, and lifted him up" (Acts 3:4, 6–7).

Another scripture story that took on new meaning after Lexi's accident is the story of Gideon in the Old Testament.

His hand is stretched out still.
—Isaiah 9:12

The children of Israel were in bondage to the Midianites when an angel of the Lord appeared unto Gideon and told him the Lord was with him. Gideon said, "Oh my Lord, if the Lord be with us, why then is all this befallen us? and where be all his miracles which our fathers told us of, saying, Did not the Lord bring us up from Egypt? but now the Lord hath forsaken us and delivered us into the hands of the Midianites" (Judges 6:13).

Yes, I thought. *Why has this befallen us? Where are the miracles that happened before?* Just as Gideon needed to have several signs, or assurances, from God before having the faith to go to battle, I realized I needed those same assurances.

The scriptures continue, "And the Lord looked upon him, and said, Go in this thy might, and thou shalt save Israel from the hand of the Midianites: have not I sent thee?" (Judges 6:14). Our family was given a similar promise—that Lexi would be saved from death and make a full recovery. These personal revelations brought comfort, yet part of me was like Gideon as he replied to the Lord, "Oh my Lord, wherewith shall I save Israel? behold, my family is poor in Manasseh, and I am the least in my father's house" (Judges 6:15).

I, too, wondered why the Lord would choose our family to perform this great miracle when so many other families have lost loved ones to untimely deaths. Our family would be considered the least in the world's view. We were not rich or powerful or famous.

Even though Gideon was told, "The Lord is with thee" (Judges 6:12), he was understandably wary that the Lord would indeed perform a miracle for his people as He had done for Moses. Would God use him to help defeat such a fearsome foe as the Midianites? Gideon wanted unshakable faith, greater courage to leave his skepticism behind, so he asked for a sign. He told the Lord, "Behold, I will put a fleece of wool in the floor; and if the dew be on the fleece only, and it be dry upon all the earth beside, then shall I know that thou wilt save Israel. . . . And it was so" (Judges 6:37–38).

> *I have fought a good fight. . . . I have kept the faith.*
> —2 Timothy 4:7

Needing that reassurance myself, I found my "signs" in the scriptures. I gained courage, and my faith grew when I read about Gideon, Elisha, Joshua, and other prophets. Elisha reminded his servant to not be afraid because "they that be with us are more than they that be with them" (2 Kings 6:16). And Joshua taught his people to "be strong and of a good courage" (Joshua 1:6).

After Gideon received signs from the Lord, he faithfully

reduced his army from thirty-two thousand to three hundred men so that "Israel [might not] vaunt themselves against [the Lord] saying, Mine own hand hath saved me" (Judges 7:2). Likewise, as I prepared to go to battle against a vast army of doctors, nurses, and therapists reinforced with their knowledge and expertise that Lexi's brain injury was too insurmountable to overcome, I felt a lot like Gideon. I have never been more grateful for these words spoken to Gideon and to all of us, "The Lord is with thee" (Judges 6:12). Now I could go forward and say, "Yes, a GCS score of three can still win when the Lord is in charge of the healing."

If Lexi's injuries had consisted of broken bones, fractured ribs, or even a concussion—but had not been life threatening—people might have focused their attention solely on Lexi and left God out of the picture. For instance, they might have said that she was healed because she was a fighter. Yet because her injuries were so severe and the doctors gave her less than one percent chance to live, the focus when she did recover was really not on Lexi and her ability to fight to survive. It was on God and His goodness and might.

This focus on God's power was where it should have been and should always be. Our family talks about this miracle using the words, "God is amazing," or, "God is a God of miracles." If someone tries to give the credit to Lexi or to the doctors, I immediately correct them and let them know that although Lexi is a fighter and a good girl and the doctors were extremely capable and did a lot to help her, in the end it was God who saw fit to extend her life for a season. We stand firmly in our faith with that conviction.

NOTE

1. "Be Still, My Soul," *Hymns*, no. 124.

Chapter Twelve

THE MIRACLE OF
LOOKING UP

The Lord God of heaven . . . shall send his angel before thee.

—Genesis 24:7

On February 28, two days after the accident, the doctor came in and tried to wake up Lexi. He called out her name loudly, over and over, to get her to open her eyes. When she didn't respond, he gave her a hard pinch under the armpit, which caused her to grimace in pain, and her eyes blinked open for a split second. Although I didn't like watching her experience pain, I was relieved to see her eyes open, even if only for a moment.

He then started tapping her thumb and asked her to give him a thumbs-up with her left hand. She opened her eyes again, and there seemed to be a slight movement in her thumb, but then her eyes closed, and she lay still. He repeated this same thing on her right side, but this time, there was no reaction. After seeing no response, he continued to pinch her harder and harder and speak to her louder and louder. After doing this several times, she finally raised the left thumb just enough so that it was obvious to all of us she understood the command.

We squealed with excitement! Just seeing this slight movement in her thumb gave us hope. It was an important milestone on her long road to recovery, but also a foreshadowing of the trials to come in her efforts to gain her abilities back. The good news spread through the hospital. Later that day, I saw the attendant who helped us the night Lexi was brought in. Before I could say a word, he gave me a thumbs-up, showing he had already heard the great news. We both were beaming!

The ICU had a rule that only two visitors were allowed into a patient's room at a time, so the members of our family had to trade off time with Lexi. Luckily, I wasn't counted as part of that number and was allowed to stay in her room and take care of her instead of only being permitted to come in occasionally like the rest of the family.

As I spent more time in her room, I began to feel disconnected from the world and could "stop, and stand still" (Doctrine and Covenants 5:34). Often, my children tried to get me to go

> *Even in the worst conditions when Joseph was sold as a slave, "the Lord was with him, [and] the Lord made all that he did to prosper in his hand." And when Joseph was thrown in prison, "the Lord was with Joseph, and shewed him mercy and gave him favour in the sight of the keeper of the prison."*
>
> —Genesis 39:3, 21

out into the waiting room to talk with the various visitors who came to the hospital to give us support and comfort. They assumed it would be good for me to get my mind off of Lexi by stepping away from the constant interruptions of therapists, nurses, and doctors, if only for a few minutes. But I couldn't leave for two reasons: first, I wanted to be right by Lexi's side at all times, and, second, staying near her allowed me to learn how to "be still, and know that [he is] God" (Psalm 46:10). Better, I felt His spirit strengthening me.

On Saturday morning, I sat communing with God, unaware of the doctors and nurses coming in and out or the beeping sound of machines monitoring her every movement. It felt good to finally have that transformation of peace seep deep into my soul. I could see the hand of God and His grace manifested in my life more clearly as I reflected on all the events that had transpired in the days previous.

> *Be still, and know that I am God. . . . The Lord of hosts is with us; the God of Jacob is our refuge.*
>
> —Psalm 46:10–11

Perhaps from an outsider's view, Lexi's hospital room would have looked sterile, dreary, and depressing. Yet it had become a temple for me. My children who took turns rotating in throughout each day thought of it as a temple as well, bringing their scriptures to study, ponder, and pray in that holy setting. JD had been reading a few articles that expanded upon the scriptures, and he was eager to share important messages with me.

After a couple of sleepless nights of me sitting by the hospital bed holding Lexi's hand, my children insisted that I drive back to our house at night to get some sleep. They promised me that they would each take shifts during the night, knowing I would not leave Lexi's side unless I knew someone would be there with her. Even though my children and their spouses were exhausted, they were still willing to sacrifice their sleep for Lexi. I was grateful for my children's offer and was impressed with the love that they showed for their little sister. But I still felt a twinge of remorse leaving her side.

However, it proved difficult for me to leave Lexi's room because I had received strength from the presence of her angelic visitors. There was great power when the seen and unseen worlds met. I had felt the angels the first night I stayed with her, and that feeling stretched on through the coming days and weeks. I felt there were many that had passed on who had come to be with Lexi, lifting some of the sorrow and bleakness from my heart. While in her room, I felt elevated spiritually by divine help, primarily from my parents who had passed on. It brought a power that seemed tangible. I whispered into the silence of the room that I needed their help, in particular for my dad to pray over Lexi. I *knew* they were there. I was blessed to linger in their presence hour after hour, to feel the calmness of the gentle spirit they brought. I learned how very thin the veil is between us and our loved ones who have passed on. And I could feel a change coming over me.

A week later, Lexi confirmed what I felt and knew. My daughter Cassidy and I asked Lexi if she remembered anything during the time when she was in the coma, particularly if someone she knew who had passed on had come to help her. She told us that Grandma and Grandpa were there (my parents) and that little children were there. About a week after that, we asked her for more details about who and what she had seen. This second time, however, she informed us that she had forgotten everything from when she was in the coma. Her memory of those events was gone. In fact, Lexi had no recollection of telling us about seeing angelic visitors. Thankfully, Cassidy had thought to record Lexi's words. Although Lexi confirmed what I felt, it didn't make my knowledge of what had happened any more sure. On the contrary, my experience with those visiting loved ones was a much more powerful witness for me; I knew they were there, and I didn't need anyone to tell me.

> And when we cried unto the Lord, he heard our voice, and sent an angel, and hath brought us forth.
> —Numbers 20:16

This is another example of how the stories I had read in the scriptures seemed to be playing out in my own life on a smaller scale. In the Old Testament, Elijah's servant had been so fearful of the impending army and was told, "Fear not: for they that be with us are more than they that be with them" (2 Kings 6:16). Then he saw "the mountain was full of horses and chariots of fire round about" coming to their aid (2 Kings 6:17). I felt the same

> Be not forgetful to entertain strangers: for thereby some have entertained angels unawares.
> —Hebrews 13:2

thing was happening on our behalf, as our room filled with an unseen army of angels helping Lexi fight for her life.

As I prepared to return home for the night, I leaned down to give Lexi a parting kiss. Then I gently brushed a strand of blonde hair away from her eyes and tucked it behind her ear. Stroking her arm, I leaned forward and whispered that I loved her. Her eyes were not open, but I believed she could hear me. I gave her one more glance before I left.

As I began my exit, I felt strength leave me. Just stepping outside of her room, there was a tangible difference in the Spirit that I felt, and, as a result, I felt alone and vulnerable. I prayed to God that His spirit would stay with me so that I could maintain the same spiritual high that I had while at Lexi's side. I didn't want to walk outside into the world because it felt almost as if I were leaving heaven. However, when I exited the hospital, the noise of the cars, coupled with the business of life, was a rude awakening. I was in the real world again.

The lingering daylight vanished, and my car was barely visible in the darkness. I pleaded with the Lord to know how I might stay in a state of comfort and peace surrounded by his "armour of light" (Romans 13:12). After I finished my prayer, these words came immediately to my mind, Marcia, look up." I did, and with the moon illuminating the sky, I saw right in front of me the most stunning array of clouds in the heavens.

It was as if God were saying to me, "I'm right here. I won't leave you. You are mine. I know you, and I am aware of what you are going through."

His voice whispered to me that His presence would be with me and that these clouds were to show His

> *Did not our heart burn within us, while he talked with us by the way?*
> —Luke 24:32

marvelous love for me. I drew in a breath as a rush of courage surged though me. My eyes started to tear, and I was filled with unspeakable joy as a heavenly light distilled upon my soul. I was reminded of the children of Israel when "the Lord went before them by day in a pillar of a cloud, to lead them the way" (Exodus 13:21). I, too, had received a glimpse into heaven through the lingering brilliance of the clouds.

The Lord has also taught others this concept of "looking up." For instance, He taught the children of Israel through Moses to look up to "a fiery serpent . . . upon a pole: and . . . every one that [was] bitten, when he looketh upon it, [lived]" (Numbers 21:8). But some would not look up because they did not believe that it would heal them. Yet the Lord promises us that if we do "lift up [our] eyes to the heavens" (Isaiah 51:6) and begin to believe in the Son of God "the Lord shall comfort Zion . . . and he will make her wilderness like Eden . . . joy and gladness shall be found therein" (Isaiah 51:3). What a small thing we are asked to do in order for our burdens to be lifted.

I continued to watch the clouds as I drove home, and the feeling of peace persisted. I became lost in thought, pondering on God's mercy given to me. The stillness of the night caused me to pause and reverently feel His arms encircling me in His love.

After that night, I continued to drive back and forth between home and the hospital each day. The first thing I would do in the golden glow of dawn was look up at the sky to see the wonder of the clouds. There seemed to be a reverence and a hush over the

> They may forget, yet will I not forget thee. Behold I have graven thee upon the palms of my hands; thy walls are continually before me.
>
> —Isaiah 49:15

city when I focused on looking up. I felt protected in its stillness from outside influences. I felt the Lord speaking to me, "Marcia, look what kind of formation I made for you today. Isn't that beautiful? I will be with you through this trial every step of the way. You just need to keep looking up." I found I couldn't wait to see what God had created for me each morning.

I still can't go outside or get into my car without first admiring the clouds. Often, as I look up at the sky above me, the grandeur of the heavens moves me to tears of gratitude and takes my breath away. No matter where we are, God has a way of showing us that He is near, if we will just look up.

Chapter Thirteen

THE MIRACLE THAT COMES THROUGH FASTING

Therefore also now, saith the Lord, turn ye even to me with all your heart, and with fasting.

—Joel 2:12

I love the scripture found in the gospel of Matthew that says, "Ask, and it shall be given you; seek, and ye shall find; knock, and it shall be opened unto you. For every one that asketh receiveth; and he that seeketh findeth; and to him that knocketh it shall be opened" (Matthew 7:7–8). It teaches us that God is always ready to help us. However, the key is whether or not we will invite Him in. I found that this particular scripture had great relevance as I prayed and fasted for Lexi during those first days in the hospital.

In the past, fasting hadn't been easy for me. Many times I

found myself counting down the hours until I was able to eat again. However, during Lexi's recovery, fasting was a welcome reprieve from the distress I was experiencing. Food actually became a burden. As each day passed without eating, I could sense I was becoming more receptive to the promptings of the Holy Spirit and learning the mind and will of God as spirit spoke to spirit. Generally, our church leaders recommend not fasting too frequently or for excessive periods of time. However, in my grief, I found myself truly unable to eat, so I chose to continue fasting.

My son Tanner was worried about me because of the stress, heartache, and sleepless nights I had faced. He also noticed that no food had been brought to me from the waiting room. He was very perceptive; no one else had realized I had not eaten for days. Each family member was only with me sporadically due to the limited number of people allowed in Lexi's room.

"Mom," he told me, "if you don't eat something, you will collapse and have to be admitted to the hospital yourself. Then we will have to take care of you as well as Lexi. You have *got* to eat! Really, Mom, you do. I'm going to go get some food for you right now."

I was touched by his perceptiveness and thoughtfulness. "Tan, I'm okay. I really am," I explained. "I'm not hungry, and I can feel the Lord fortifying me. I promise I will eat if my body needs to, but right now I am fine. I don't know how . . . but I am." Truly, I had felt a power beyond my own strengthening me, and it was a marvelous spiritual experience.

But Tanner was relentless, and on Saturday morning, he came in again. "Okay, Mom," he said, "I'm not going to let you do this any longer. I'm bringing you some food."

I had no desire for food, but I could tell he was not going to give this up, so I said, "Okay, Tan, I'll eat, but please give me until noon?" I said this to pacify him because I didn't think he would remember to come back.

But just like clockwork, he appeared in the room at twelve o'clock with a plate of food. "You promised," he reminded me and handed me a plate overflowing with an assortment of food.

Despite his kindness and my desire not to offend him, I couldn't bring myself to eat. I looked at him rather sheepishly. "I know I promised, but can you just give me a few more hours before I eat?"

Sensing my yearnings to fast, he agreed to wait, but he was insistent we come up with another time. "Okay then, what time? Two?"

I quickly agreed. "Yes," I promised, "by two o'clock I will be ready."

He looked at me sternly but kindly. "This time it's a promise, and you can't break it."

I knew exactly what time it was when a few hours later, Tanner walked through the doorway with a new plate of food. He said firmly but lovingly, "Okay, you gave your word. It's time to eat!"

He placed the food down by my chair and left the room. Just as he left, a doctor came in, so I slipped the meal behind some books to get it out of the way while the doctor talked to me. A half hour later, Tanner emerged again. His eyes scanned the room and quickly saw the lunch was gone. He beamed, assuming I'd eaten the food, and praised me: "You ate it. Way to go. I'm so proud of you."

Howbeit this kind goeth not out but by prayer and fasting.
—Matthew 17:21

For a minute our roles were reversed, and I was the child. I didn't have the heart to tell him I hadn't eaten, but I couldn't lie either. I slid back the stack of books, revealing the hidden plate of food and sheepishly told him, "Sorry, Tan, I haven't taken a bite yet, but I will."

However, deep inside I knew that I couldn't, at least not then . . . maybe the next day. Tanner didn't remind me again about the food. An understanding came to his heart that I needed to fast and that the Lord would take care of me. But Tanner's desire to look out for my physical welfare made me feel fortunate and cared for. It was the perfect preface to the Sabbath, a day of community fasting and prayer for Lexi, in which every heart would be as one.

Fasting is a commandment that has been practiced by God's people throughout time. In the book of Esther, I studied the story of the Jew Mordecai. He refused to bow to Haman, so Haman arranged a decree to kill all the Jews in the kingdom. Mordecai asked Queen Esther, whom he had raised after her parents' deaths, to go before the king in behalf of all the Jews. But "all the . . . people of the king's provinces [knew] that whosoever [should] come unto the king into the inner court, who is not called, there is one law of his to put him to death, except such to whom the king shall hold out the golden sceptre, that he may live . . . Then Esther [gave] this answer, Go, gather together all the Jews . . . and fast ye for me, and neither eat nor drink three days, night or day: I also . . . will fast . . . and if I perish, I perish" (Esther 4:11, 15–16). There is great power in fasting; after the Jews fasted as a community, Queen Esther came into the presence of the king and was welcome. The Jews were not killed.

At a time of such hardship, the Lord could not have given me greater support than the solace that comes from fasting. I knew in my heart that this was a pivotal day in Lexi's progress. That Sabbath day, thousands of people fasted for Lexi, including her friends, extended family, neighbors, children, and people she had never met from all over the world. The leader of Lexi's college congregation organized a continuous fast on the night of the accident. Every day after that, until Sunday night, he arranged to have a several hundred people take turns fasting for her.

Our neighbors asked our community to fast for Lexi. In the church that we attended, they wanted to have a special prayer for her at the end the meeting. After hearing this, I was overwhelmed with gratitude. I felt strongly that we should ask the leader of our congregation to have the entire congregation kneel for that prayer instead of sitting in the pews. I felt it needed to be done this way as we approached the God of heaven, asking for such an incredible miracle. Doug didn't feel like he should bother him with this request, but at my insistence, he was kind enough to call back to ask him. He was more than happy and willing to do this for our family and for Lexi.

Many of our friends and neighbors who went to that meeting said they could feel the presence of angels when they entered the chapel. Others told me that they had never been to a more sacred church meeting in their entire lives. Even little children told their parents they believed that Lexi would be healed! It seemed the whole community was ablaze with the fire of faith and testimony, believing that if they did their part, Lexi could be healed.

As our family prayed and fasted for Lexi on that Sunday, we had the most spiritual uplifting day. The family went to church that morning in the hospital, while I stayed with Lexi. A few of my children felt

> Verily my sabbaths ye shall keep: for it is a sign between me and you . . . that ye may know that I am the Lord that doth sanctify you.
>
> —Exodus 31:13

113

touched by the Spirit to share their love of the Savior and of His power in the meeting, which was the perfect start for the incredible spiritual experiences to follow. While we fasted, prayed, and read the scriptures during the day, we felt God especially near us. Despite being in a hospital setting, all the women in our family managed to find dresses to wear, and the men found suits, bringing an added spirit of reverence to the Sabbath. Never in my life had I felt the spirit of the Savior flow so freely in my being as I did that fast Sunday.

Throughout the day, the family continued their usual rotation of two people in the room at a time to see Lexi. However, at about four o'clock, family members began coming in Lexi's room without waiting for the other family members to leave. It was as if the Spirit was drawing us to be there together.

While I was standing next to Lexi, holding her hand, she gently blinked opened her eyes and kept them open for the first time. Previously, though they had taken her off the sedation medication, she hadn't opened her eyes longer than a minute or two before closing them again. I could not remove my gaze from her face. I suggested that we sing some hymns to her, sensing that music would be the cure. Everyone agreed, and we sang "I Need Thee Every Hour," "Abide with Me!" "Come Thou Fount of Every Blessing," and other hymns that we loved and knew would bring peace to Lexi.

> *Fear ye not, stand still, and see the salvation of the Lord, which he will shew to you to day. . . . The Lord shall fight for you.*
>
> —Exodus 14:13–14

We were surprised that after every song we sang, her eyes remained wide open, watching our every move. So we continued to sing. As this was happening, Lexi's sister Kelsi raced to the waiting room to gather the few stragglers and notify them to come and see Lexi with her eyes open. As we huddled together in that small ICU room, we were blessed that not one member of the hospital staff asked us to leave. This was remarkable because we have such a large family. As each family member entered the room, Lexi gingerly raised her hand and waved to them. My eyes blinked, tears pooling and spilling onto the floor as we started to see this miracle unfold before our eyes.

We sang for nearly an hour, and, as we did, the Spirit entered the room in greater abundance. It was as if we were experiencing a piece of heaven. As we sang, Lexi slowly moved her gaze from one person to the next until she had looked at every person in the room. At that moment, we felt that she knew who we were and that she comprehended the situation. She even tried to touch her sister Shae with her toes when she saw her at the end of her bed. We also knew that family who had passed on had joined us in the room. It seemed even "the morning stars sang together, and all the sons of God shouted for joy" (Job 38:7). In this moment, I felt such incredible love for Lexi, for my family, and especially for the Lord.

After singing, the most remarkable and unforgettable thing happened. With every eye locked on her, Lexi hand-signed, "I love you," moving her outstretched arm around in a circle to let each of us see. Then she repeated the sign again with her other hand in the opposite direction. A hush fell over the room. My heart quickened, and I hardly dared to breathe; we felt we were on hallowed ground. Besides the sniffs and hiccups caused by tears, silence penetrated the space. The Spirit whispered to us that we were literally eyewitnesses to a miracle.

Tears flowed freely, and God's graciousness overwhelmed us. The strength of His love had been felt from the tops of our heads to the bottom of our feet. God had heard our pleas and accepted our fast. By His power we felt and saw with our own eyes that he brought our daughter and sister, Lexi, back to life.

How was it possible? I was still trying to take it all in and to fully comprehend what had just taken place. She was completely aware of everyone around her when only an hour ago she was still in a coma-like state. Our hearts were swollen with joy. My daughter-in-law Mandy summed it up well when she wrote, "The Spirit was so powerful and seemed to coat every inch of the room. I literally felt it radiate through my entire body."

> So we fasted and besought our God for this: and he was entreated of us.
>
> —Ezra 8:23

After Lexi signed, "I love you," she reached her hand up to Parker, who was standing closest to her. He took her hand and held it for a minute before she let go and reached for the person standing next to him. She continued reaching out her hand until she had grasped the hand of each family member individually. It was as if she wanted each of us to know of her love for us. The silence in the room deepened, and we marveled over the wonder we had experienced. No one wanted to leave the sweetness of the room, but because of the hospital policy, the family exited, wrapped in a newness of life. As each person left, Lexi gave a slight smile and waved goodbye. We learned the truth of Isaish's promise that after we fast then "thou shalt call, and the Lord shall answer; and then thou shalt cry, and he sall say, Here I am" (Isaiah 58:9).

I've always pondered how it would feel to live in Christ's day and to see His miracles. But through this experience my soul burned bright with the knowledge that I had personally seen Christ's power. Joshua's words had literally been fulfilled to us when he wrote, "Sanctify yourselves: for . . . the Lord will do wonders among you" (Joshua 3:5). And we did rejoice, and "the peace of God [did] rule in [our] hearts" (Colossians 3:15) because of the things we saw. Our God is indeed a God of miracles. Jesus had loosened the bands of death, and I felt to shout praises to heaven.

The next day, my niece Angela told me about her daughters, Mary and Emma, who were just four and eight years old. She and her husband told them on that particular Sunday that their family was going to hold a fast for Lexi. They also explained that fasting meant to sacrifice food and water in order to call down a blessing from heaven. After learning this, Emma and Mary decided that they wanted

> [Jesus] said unto them, Suffer the little children to come unto me, and forbid them not: for of such is the kingdom of God. . . . And he took them up in his arms, put his hands upon them, and blessed them.
>
> —Mark 10:14, 16

to fast for the first time with their parents. Later that evening, after they had completed their fast, the family read the post on the "Pray for Lexi" Facebook page that shared how Lexi had awoken from her coma that evening. After reading about the amazing miracle that had happened, Mary and Emma were astonished. Mary turned to her mom and whispered, "I didn't know a little kid, like me, could help a big person."

Likewise, our hearts were touched as we were told of the many children and adults from different parts of the world who fasted for Lexi and who took it upon themselves to help bear our burden. We were humbled by their boldness, their believing hearts, and their connection to heaven. The glow of their testimonies is best described by this scripture, "If thou canst believe, all things are possible" (Mark 9:23). The Spirit also confirmed to

them that Lexi's miracle was a result of their fasting and their faith in the tender mercies of a loving God.

After this amazing miracle, we assumed that this was the end of our trial, for our Lexi had been brought back to us. Yet we would soon find out that the Lord wanted to teach our family many other lessons. We would discover how many more deep rivers we needed to wade through in order to refine our characters.

Chapter Fourteen

THE MIRACLE TO ACCEPT OUR TRIALS

The Lord is my rock, and my fortress, and my deliverer; The God of my rock; in him will I trust: he is my shield, and the horn of my salvation, my high tower, and my refuge, my savior.

—2 Samuel 22:2–3

My son McKay shared some of his thoughts after Lexi came out of the coma. He wrote:

We have followed Lexi's story in the media with amazement as it has caught not only local, but also worldwide interest. Articles about her have been published in faraway places like Nigeria, Brazil, and the United Kingdom. As I read these articles, I have been drawn to the comments of the readers. I wondered if other people would also believe the miracle. By and large, the comments were positive and supportive; however, there was also a common thread in which people expressed a very thoughtful concern for others who have

119

suffered and haven't recovered. Their question in a nutshell is, "What of those whose pleas to God have seemingly gone unanswered? If God is a caring, loving God, wouldn't He love them like He loves Lexi?"

I have pondered this very real and genuine concern and wanted to share what I have learned. First, I don't presume to know why God chooses to heal and bless some while letting others suffer tremendously. It is indeed hard to fathom how a caring, loving God would permit His children to experience pain and heartache. But to all those who have watched others suffer or suffered themselves and wondered why God allowed it, I would direct them to our Exemplar and Savior, Jesus Christ. Just as we are allowed to suffer, He whom God called his "Beloved Son" was allowed to suffer more than anyone who has ever walked the face of the earth. Christ describes His own suffering in this way: "My God, my God, why hast thou forsaken me?" (Matthew 27:46).

It appears that even Christ himself didn't completely understand the need for all the pain that lay ahead of Him as he knelt in the Garden of Gethsemane and petitioned His Father to "remove this cup" (Luke 22:42). Did this mean that Christ was unloved by His Father? No! He lived and experienced His Father's love almost every moment of His life and sought every day to teach all of us exactly what this pure love was and how to achieve it.

Yet God did have His reasons to allow such travail and agony: through Christ's suffering, He atoned for our sins. Additionally, Paul testified, "That he would grant you, according to the riches of his glory, to be strengthened with might by his Spirit in the inner man; That Christ may dwell in your hearts by faith" (Ephesians 3:16–17). Notice that he didn't say that the trials would be removed or taken away but that we would be supported through them. And we saw this take place for our family. When

Lexi was in the coma, our family put our trust in God, and we received support! We received it in the form of comfort and peace through our Savior. We were able to be consoled by Christ because He had suffered and experienced our pain; therefore, He knew how to console us in our sorrows: "For in that he himself hath suffered being tempted, he is able to succour them that are tempted" (Hebrews 2:18).

Many of the trials and pain we experience are the result of living in an imperfect world and are not caused by God. But just as our Savior, Jesus Christ, is able to lift and strengthen us in our infirmities because of the afflictions that He bore, we can also become more capable of lifting others when we go through trials and tribulations. Moreover, God shows His love to us by lifting us and supporting us through our trials. He often accomplishes this act of love through the means of other people who have also suffered or gone through similar trials and, therefore, can offer empathy, encouragement, and a shoulder to lean on. I ultimately believe that Lexi was healed so she can be the means of showing the goodness of God to others. However, even if she had not been made whole, I know that we would have still received His support and peace, and eventually my family could and would have been healed through His marvelous gift.

> Now no chastening for the present seemeth to be joyous, but grievous: nevertheless afterward it yieldeth the peaceable fruit of righteousness.
> —Hebrews 12:11

Like McKay, my heart has also gone out to those who have not had prayers answered as directly as our prayers for Lexi were. Yet, I feel I can understand a little of what some are going through because our oldest daughter, Shae, has not been healed of her afflictions.

She was born with multiple disabilities. She is deaf, has cerebral palsy, and has some mental deficiencies. Despite our prayers, she continues to struggle with this challenges.

Lexi has seen firsthand how lonely life can be when your body doesn't work properly, especially if that person is deaf and isolated from the hearing world. Therefore, learning sign language was extremely important to her. Even though she learned some sign language at home, she wanted to be more proficient at it. Her high school didn't offer a sign language class, and her principal refused to add it, but Lexi was undeterred and asked any interested students to sign a petition to get the class included in the curriculum. Because of the overwhelming amount of signatures, the principal's heart was swayed, and the class was added. From this experience, Lexi's American Sign Language skills significantly improved, and this helped to deepen her relationship with her sister.

Although Lexi was fifteen years younger than Shae, it became apparent to Lexi at an early age that Shae didn't have any friends besides her family. Like the rest of her siblings, Lexi colored pictures and played simple games with her and helped to feed and dress her. Shae would then lovingly pat Lexi's head or sign "I love you." Because of Shae's limitations, many times, she would take her frustrations out on the family. Sometimes she would rip out chunks of Lexi's hair or bite or hit her. Despite the sting of Shae's anger, Lexi was quick to forgive.

Over the years since Shae's birth, we have learned to trust in the Lord, knowing He knows what is best for us. He listens to our prayers even when those petitions aren't answered the way *we* want. Looking back, we have gained wisdom from the trials that have been a part of our lives and have come to recognize that our prayers were unanswered not because God does not love us but because He trusts us to be faithful in the midst of our challenges.

In order for our family to be reminded of this principle—to trust in the Lord's wisdom daily—we have three words stenciled above the doorway in our living room: *But if not.* These words come from a scriptural account in the book of Daniel.

Nebuchadnezzar had constructed a great image and commanded the people that "at what time ye hear the sound of the . . . musick, ye fall down and worship the golden image . . . And whoso falleth not down and worshippeth shall the same hour be cast into the midst of a burning fiery furnace. Therefore at that time, when all the people heard the sound . . . of musick, all the people . . . fell down and worshipped the golden image" (Daniel 3:5–7). However, three young men—Shadrach, Meshach, and Abed-nego—were steadfast and immovable in their beliefs and remained standing. When they were brought before the king, he demanded, "And who is that God that shall deliver you out of my hands?" (Daniel 3:15).

The faith of these young men shone bright in their resolved response: "If it be so, our God whom we serve is able to deliver us from the burning fiery furnace, and he will deliver us out of thy hand, O king. *But if not*, be it known unto thee, O king, that we will not serve thy gods, nor worship the golden image which thou hast set up" (Daniel 3:17–18; italics added). They were then bound, fully clothed, and thrown into the flames.

However, as the king looked into the flames, he saw that they walked freely, unbound and unhurt, and that a fourth person was with them. Then they came forth from the furnace with their hair and clothing untouched. Not even "the smell of fire had passed on them" (Daniel 3:27).

> *He will deliver us out of thy hand, O king. But if not . . . we will not serve thy gods.*
>
> —Daniel 3:17–18

Can we have faith in God's plan for us like Shadrach, Meshach, and Abednego, even if it means our reward won't come to us in this life? Will we believe God will deliver us from cancer, sickness, or depression? *But if not*, can we still trust His plan for us? If our teenagers are made fun of and ridiculed because of their beliefs, will they say, "Our God will deliver us, *but if not*, we will remain true"? When we are friendless or lonely and feel forsaken or afraid can we say, "Our God will deliver us, *but if not*, we will trust in our Savior"? When things don't go as planned and we don't receive the rewards, medals, promotions, and honors we feel we deserve, can we say, "*But if not*, we will have faith in God"?

Some of the trials we endure in life can last for years, and we may wonder if they will ever be lifted from us. Sometimes when we cry out for help, we may question whether our pleadings are landing on deaf ears. The prophet Moses was told to "say unto Pharaoh . . . Let my son go, that he may serve me" (Exodus 4:22–23). How did the Lord answer Moses? Were his people let free with Pharaoh's hardened heart dissolving into love? No, it was completely the opposite. Life for the Israelites was made far worse when Pharaoh demanded, "Ye shall no more give the people straw to make brick, as heretofore: let them go and gather straw for themselves. . . . Let there more work be laid upon the men, that they may labour therein" (Exodus 5:7, 9).

I'm sure many of us can relate to having a prayer answered in this manner, where the very thing that we are praying to be relieved of becomes even harder to bear. "Behold, I have refined thee, but not with silver; I have chosen thee in the furnace of affliction" (Isaiah 48:10).

But, like Moses, can we do anything less than to follow God's counsel and enter our own unknown wildernesses?

I have learned that as I follow God's instructions, He always leads me from the darkest hour of night into the dawn of His morning light. Each time I have trusted and obeyed, my faith has grown stronger, and I have been reminded that God sees the big picture, while I only see the here and now.

Chapter Fifteen

THE MIRACLE THAT CHRIST HEALS THE BROKENHEARTED

And forgive us our debts, as we forgive our debtors.

—Matthew 6:12

On Monday, March 3, five days after the accident, I arrived at the hospital early in the morning. My son Tanner and his wife Mandy had stayed the night with Lexi, and I finally felt rested after having my first peaceful sleep since the accident. When I came into Lexi's room, Tanner and Mandy were anxiously waiting for me.

"Mom, you would not believe what was delivered to Lexi's room last night," Tanner announced.

Mandy hurried across the room and picked up an envelope from the table and handed it to me. "It's from the driver of the car that hit Lexi," she said in a seemingly reverent voice. "A nurse brought it to our room late last night."

My heart sank. Up until that point, our family had not been able to find or contact the driver to let him know that we were not angry and didn't hold him responsible. I felt it was our duty to reach out to him and not the other way around, knowing he would have been scared to reach out to us. I felt horrible knowing he had suffered needlessly when he was also in desperate need of support. I felt our family should have done more to contact him.

I opened the folded up piece of paper and began reading. In the letter he penned,

> I want you to know how heartbroken and sorrowful I feel about what has happened to Lexi. My heart just aches every single day, knowing what has happened to such an amazing daughter, sister, and friend. Since the accident, I have been endlessly fasting and praying for miracles to take place on her behalf. I have felt on a very personal level the amount of love God has for Lexi and the rest of your family. With each update on Lexi's condition, I am humbled by your unity and faith in Jesus Christ and his ability to work miracles in our lives. With all the conviction of my soul. I want you to know how sorry I feel that this accident took place, and I pray you have felt my prayers pleading with our Father in Heaven to comfort Lexi and to comfort all of you during this difficult time. I will continue to pray for Lexi and the entire Hansen family and to comfort your family.

He hath sent me to heal the brokenhearted.
—Luke 4:18

My heart ached for him as I learned of the sorrow and pain that he had suffered, especially when reading these words that he wrote: "In my own life, I take pride in and feel so much joy in making people around me feel good, but to know the sadness and grief that has come from this accident has shaken me to the very core." Although it was a different type of grief than what we were experiencing, I'm sure he cried out that first night, as we did, "Where is God my maker" (Job 35:10). "How long, O Lord, holy and true" (Revelations 6:10). Oh, how I felt for him! I thought about how if this had been one of my own sons, I would have wanted a kind and tender person reaching out to him.

I could tell by his letter that he also had a strong foundation in the Lord. One of the last things he wrote was very powerful: "I know that through our Savior Jesus Christ, we can ALL be healed." I love how he said "we," knowing that our family's hearts needed to be healed in addition to Lexi's body. But in a much larger scope, his words also remind us that no matter what struggle we are going through in life, it is only the Savior that can change us.

Later he expressed to me how reading the Facebook page we had set up for Lexi had only made his grief worse. As he read about her life, he realized he had hit a girl who was not only loved and respected by many, but who was also devoted to God. She was good, kind, and loving, and he was the one responsible for potentially taking her life.

At the bottom of the letter, he signed his name, Karson, and left his phone number and email address. Mandy had the impression that she should send him an email right away to let him know that our family had been praying and fasting for him in addition to Lexi. I'm sure Karson had been extremely nervous sending the letter, not knowing how it would be received. And he had taken a leap of faith by leaving his name and number at the end.

After I finished reading the letter, it was just barely 6 a.m., so I decided it was still too early to call him. I waited impatiently until about 7:30 a.m., but when I called, no one picked up the phone. I waited another half hour and called again, yet there was still no answer. This time I decided to leave a voice mail.

In the message, I let Karson know that we were not upset with him. I told him accidents just happen and that I believed this misfortune had happened for a reason. I let him know that I believed this was all part of God's plan, as our community and the world were hungering for knowledge that God still answers prayers. I believed we all needed to be part of a miracle to strengthen our faith and to be reminded that God is still a God of miracles. I expressed to him how sorry I was for the anguish he was experiencing and that I knew he was chosen for his strength of character to go through this tragedy—to be the catalyst to bring about the love that seemed to be overflowing in the community. I then asked him if he would meet us in the hospital waiting room to have dinner together that night. I expressed again how sorry I was for the pain he must have been going through, and then I hung up.

> *Now therefore be not grieved, nor angry with [yourself] . . . for God did send [you] . . . to preserve life . . . by a great deliverance.*
>
> —Genesis 45:5, 7

All things considered, I didn't think he would call me back, so I waited another hour and called again. This time he answered the phone, and I reiterated what I had said previously in my voice mail. He told me he thought it was probably me when I had called the first time, but he had been too frightened to answer until after I had left the message. And he expressed his willingness to meet us for dinner that evening.

That night was the first time I had gone out into the waiting room since the accident, but I felt I needed to be there to let Karson know of my love for him. My son Tanner waited for him by the elevator doors and then led him over to where our family was.

Karson entered the foyer with fear and trepidation. He arrived dressed in a suit and tie, carrying with him a bouquet of flowers for Lexi and a box of gourmet cupcakes for the family. I jumped to my feet to greet him and gave him a big hug. He felt like family from the first time I saw him. He fit right in. I could tell from his countenance that he was a good person. He was, of course, extremely nervous and hesitant. In fact, when I invited him to sit down and eat with us, he was candid in his reply: "I'm too nervous; there is no way I could eat anything," his voice strained with emotion. His body stiff, he shifted his weight, looking uncomfortable. His eyes seemed to reveal a helplessness, a longing to go back in time.

> *I have seen thy tears:*
> *behold, I will heal thee.*
> —2 Kings 20:5

After introducing him to the family, I jokingly said, "Okay, now I hope you remembered everyone's names." Although we have nine children, there were twenty-one of us together when counting the grandkids. Yet, surprisingly, he remembered quite a few names.

After the introductions, Karson sat down and talked to my children while I hurried back to be with Lexi. A great relief washed over him as he told his side of the story and what he went through that night, seeing Lexi's lifeless body lying on the pavement. He expressed to them the horror he felt realizing he might have killed her. He said he took pride in making people around him feel good and had always tried to lead a good life. To know that he could have caused so much grief and sorrow was something he couldn't bear. He reiterated that he would never, ever hurt anyone intentionally.

Karson had not been speeding the night when his car hit Lexi, but the way that the intersection was designed made it difficult for him to see her until she was directly in front of him. We also found out that the intersection was poorly lit that evening.

In fact, a few nights after the accident, two police officers came to the hospital to inform us of the details that had transpired that evening. They told us that there were only three lights working in that vicinity despite the fact that it was dusk. The officers also mentioned to us that there had been several other accidents at that same location in recent years, yet when they had approached city leaders about fixing the problem, their pleas were met with silence. The police were hoping that with Lexi's accident, the city would take note and do something.

While Karson visited with the family, he also shared a tender mercy he was given the night of the accident. He went to talk to a leader in his church about what had happened. Unbeknownst to him, that man had also hit someone in his youth who had died from her injuries. Of all the people Karson could have gone to for comfort and counsel, the Lord placed him directly across from a man who could truly understand his pain and knew exactly what he was going through.

That night, Karson reminded me of Joshua in the scriptures, as Joshua exhorts us many times to "be strong and of a good courage" (Joshua 1:6). It took a lot of courage for Karson to not only come to dinner, but also to write the letter in the first place. Later, he told us that his walk down the hospital corridors to

> I trust in the mercy of God for ever and ever.
> —Psalm 52:8

the security station to deliver the letter was the longest and most difficult trek he'd ever made in his entire life.

A few days later, after our first introduction, Karson visited me again at the hospital. This time when I stepped out of Lexi's room to greet him in the waiting room, he was not wearing a suit and tie but a pink shirt. It was like meeting a different person; his eyes were bright and his countenance dramatically changed to

> The hope of the righteous shall be gladness.
> —Proverbs 10:28

one filled with joy, happiness, and hope. That was the key: *hope.* He believed that his future could be bright, and he was no longer weighed down by this tragic incident. I could tell just by looking at his glowing smile that a burden had been lifted from his shoulders.

The only other time I left the ICU to visit with someone was the night I met with Karson's parents. I was told they were in the waiting room wanting to meet me. I felt compelled to talk with them as I had with Karson, knowing that their hearts needed healing as well.

They were waiting in a private area by Lexi's room; their earnest and solemn demeanor suggested to me they were overcome with grief, despair, and guilt over something that was not their fault or their son's fault. Sorrow filled their eyes and apprehensiveness showed clearly on their faces, wondering how they might be received. I stepped up to Karson's dad, who was closest to me, and gave him a big bear hug and then turned to his weeping mom, who stood with her head bowed. I embraced her and told her how sorry I was for their pain. Tears continued to flow down her cheeks as she responded in what seemed a sense of disbelief to what I had just said.

She looked at me and said with gentleness in her voice, "Here you are comforting us, and we are the ones that should be comforting you."

> And Esau ran to meet him, and embraced him, and fell on his neck, and kissed him: and they wept.
>
> —Genesis 33:4

But I knew the reason I could reach out to them was not because of any greatness in my character. In fact, I could tell immediately upon seeing them that they were righteous and exceptional individuals. I could be strong and at peace at that moment only because God had surrounded and blessed me with a multitude of angels who had strengthened me in countless ways during the previous week. Those angels helped me attain new heights that I couldn't have reached on my own. They purified my soul, enlarged my understanding, and healed my wounded heart.

I reaffirmed to them that I knew this was all part of God's plan. I firmly believed God had chosen Karson to go through such adversity because of the goodness of his heart and his strength of testimony. Tears gathered in my eyes when I told them of the many miracles that had happened daily since the accident and of the attending angels at her side—experiences I had not shared with anyone else besides my children, yet I felt strongly they needed to hear. It was a warm and emotional meeting between three hearts, each of which had been broken and then mended through the healing power of Christ's Atonement.

Chapter Sixteen

THE MIRACLE TO PRESS ON WITH COURAGE

Fear ye not, stand still, and see the salvation of the Lord, which he will shew to you to day . . . The Lord shall fight for you, and ye shall hold your peace.

—Exodus 14:13–14

After the day of rejoicing on Sunday, we were not prepared for the complications that set in after Lexi awoke from her coma. It was a bitter pill to swallow. It was a long and grueling day emotionally and physically. I had to remind myself that this was just part of life with its ups and downs. Our role was to continue to trust God through it all.

Lexi was extubated, meaning that she had shown enough improvement for her breathing tube to be removed. I was surprised and overjoyed that she was progressing quickly. The breathing tube was replaced with a breathing mask that was only needed every few hours. This was a big step! I was glad the tube came out because it had been pressing against her swollen lip and had made a huge dent in her lip that I knew must be quite painful. Because of the impression the tube had left, her smile was always just a half smile for several weeks. Her vocal cords were scratched and swollen from the tube having been down her throat as well. My heart hurt as I sat and watched what she had to go through. I leaned forward and stroked her arm reassuringly.

She was able to answer some questions in a raspy, barely audible whisper, but her voice was so quiet when she spoke, we couldn't always decipher what she wanted to say. It was frustrating because we wanted to know how much she comprehended mentally, but her speech was usually unintelligible. However, because she knew sign language, she was able to express her needs in that manner when she had the strength to do so, which wasn't often. One night when she was thirsty, she signed "water," and later, when she was asked what her name was, she finger-spelled, "Lexi."

If all these problems were not bad enough, they informed me that she had also caught pneumonia in one lung, and they were worried that it might spread to her other lung. The respiratory therapist came in every few hours with a big breathing mask that formed a mist that, when inhaled, helped her with her breathing difficulties. At other times, the therapist would rotate the mask with a vest that served as a ventilator and helped to loosen the mucous that had settled in her lungs. It would vibrate her rib cage and help to make her cough. As the phlegm loosened, it would be suctioned out, which allowed her airways to clear and helped her breathe better.

Lexi hated this, of course, and would cry out in pain and try to grab the tube from the nurse's hands, because it would irritate her throat until it became inflamed and raw. I grimaced and felt my knees go weak as I watched her suffer, but I willed my tears not to escape in order to be strong for her.

She seemed to do much better and endure the horror when I gently stroked her forehead with my fingers over and over; it was the only thing that seemed to soothe her. That Monday and the next couple of days were some of the hardest for Lexi personally because she was out of the coma and could feel the pain from the accident. But we knew that she "[could] do all things through Christ which strengtheneth [her]" (Philippians 4:13).

> The Lord gave, and the Lord hath taken away; blessed be the name of the Lord.
>
> —Job 1:21

Right after one of these treatments for her pneumonia, one of our favorite nurses came in and scolded me for having too many people and too much noise in Lexi's room. I turned around and stared at her. Could she really mean what she just said? I was surprised not only by her curt tone but also because I felt we had been obeying the rules, conversing mostly through whispers and allowing only two people in her room at one time. In fact, at the exact moment when she came in, the only other person in the room besides me was my oldest son, McKay, who was reading his scriptures in the corner of the room.

I kindly asked the nurse to be softer with her words because there were angels in the room helping Lexi who would depart if there was contention. But her eyes narrowed, and she insisted that we weren't obeying the rules. I had no energy for a battle of wills and had to let it go. She had always been kind and cheerful, so I wondered what triggered the episode. Maybe her supervisor had admonished her for allowing our entire family in Lexi's room to sing to her the night before.

Whether she had been reprimanded or was just having a bad day, I don't know, but as soon as she left the room, I broke into tears because of the negative spirit that was brought needlessly in the room. I had not cried like that at any other time since arriving at the hospital. It was like a dam had broken and there was no way to stop it.

As I wept, I was surprised to see Lexi extend her arm out to me, looking at me steadily. I didn't realize that she was awake and aware of what was happening around her. She couldn't talk, but managed to mouth, "Sorry, Mom." Her eyes said it all, and they pierced my soul with tenderness and love. I reached out and took hold of her hand, stifling my tears and forcing a smile for her sake.

When she drifted off to sleep, I sank back down in my chair, and my shoulders started to shake, tears coming afresh. I buried my face in my hands and sobbed uncontrollably for over an hour, until I had run out of tears and my eyes stung. My strength drained from me. I needed my daughter to heal, and I knew that the contention would delay her healing.

One nurse saw me cry and sat down next to me stroking my back, telling me it would be all right. Her kindness was soothing. I'm sure part of the reason for the flood of tears was the release of tension that had built up since the accident. I was spent from the emotionally exhausting whirlwind of the past week. I felt I had done well suppressing my feelings, yet the steady stream of tears found an escape at last. Sometimes I felt like "the battle was before and behind" (2 Chronicles 13:14) as I struggled with my concerns for Lexi and dealt with outside issues. Yet despite these hurdles, I still felt like the wind did never cease to blow toward "the land of promise" (Hebrews 11:9), because Lexi continued to make baby steps to recovery.

The doctor came in soon after I stopped crying to check on Lexi. He pointed to me and asked her who I was. I was worried that she might not remember me. However, in the slightest of whispers, she barely made out the word, "Mom." The realization of what she had said hit me with power. I was elated. Moments like this helped bring brightness to long, tedious, and sometimes heart-wrenching days of despair. I couldn't help bending down to lightly kiss her forehead, pulling her blanket around her shoulders.

Before the doctor left, he said with a compassionate smile, "She's a miracle, just remember that," as he lifted his head upward in emphasis. Nodding my head, my hand found my heart. My eyes locked with his, and a testimony was shared.

Just then, Tanner cheerfully sauntered in and asked Lexi how Grandma and Grandpa were doing, referring to my parents who had passed away a few years before. I was half startled to see her open her eyes and give him a thumbs up.

Though her speech was slurred and not readily understandable, the next few days Lexi answered questions about her name, date of birth,

For the joy of the Lord is your strength.
—Nehemiah 8:10

where she was going to school, and about her siblings—and with eight siblings, that's no small task. During our rounds of questions, JD threw in one of his own and said, "Who's your favorite brother?" Of course, he thought she would say his name since he

141

had asked the question, but Lexi, in a scarcely detectable voice, mumbled, "Parker," causing us to chuckle at JD's expense. But we knew it was true; Lexi and Parker were closest in age, giving them a special bond.

While we were talking, I happened to glance over at Lexi and noticed her fiddling with something. But because her back was toward me, I assumed she was playing with her hospital wristband. The doctors had restrained Lexi's arms while she was in the coma so she wouldn't reach up and take out her tubes. Within seconds however of her fiddling, a loud beeping noise invaded the space, interrupting the monotonous humming of machines.

I whirled around and leaped to my feet as a nurse dashed into the room. It was then that we saw Lexi had unscrewed the blood pressure cables. The nurse was astonished because she had never seen a restrained patient with the dexterity to undo such tiny screws. Lexi was not happy when the nurse pulled the restraints on Lexi's arms a little tighter so that she had less flexibility to harm herself.

I again touched the side of Lexi's forehead—one of the few unscathed places on her face—and tenderly brushed it with the tips of my fingers, soothing her back to sleep. She peered at me lovingly under her dark long lashes, smiling slightly with her eyes.

That week, Lexi also got her catheter out, but she refused to go to the bathroom in a bedpan. It would take three people to pick her up and put her on a movable toilet by her bed. The first time I realized she would not use the bedpan, I was sitting in the corner of her room when, without warning, she sat straight up and swung her legs dangerously off the side of the bed. I leaped to my feet and grabbed her before she fell onto the floor while frantically searching for the call button to get help.

I shudder to think what would have happened if I had not

been in the room at that time, because she was hooked up to several machines and could not even stand by herself. But in that instance, she seemed to have superhuman strength. The rest of the day, she would lay in bed, barely able to move her limbs, let alone pull herself into a sitting position. The nurse's jaw dropped when she reached the room and saw Lexi sitting up, legs draped over the side of the bed. We were both grateful a crisis had been averted.

The days blended together that week. On one afternoon, I had just stepped outside the room to talk with a visitor when Lexi pulled her feeding tube partway out. When I came back in, creamy white liquid was coming out of her nose, which caused her to have a coughing attack. I soon realized that the fluid was formula

> *Be strong and of a good courage; be not afraid . . . for the Lord thy God is with thee.*
> —Joshua 1:9

that had escaped from the feeding tube and was now going down her throat. Lexi winced in pain, tears streaking down her cheeks when the nurse had to pull out the feeding tube the rest of the way. I reached for her hand and squeezed it tight to help her deal with the pain, biting my lower lip so I would not cry. It was difficult to watch her suffer daily on top of everything she'd already gone through.

Despite these challenges, it was satisfying to see Lexi move around more, considering that she had been lying motionless while in a coma, and I felt a growing sense of comfort. One day that week, she lifted her left leg up and flopped it back down on the bed several times in a row. Her eyes were closed, but in an attempt to get her to move her limbs on her right side, I said,

"Wow, Lex, you can move your left leg so high. Can you move your right leg too?"

I was surprised and delighted when she lifted her right leg barely off the sheet, because I didn't think she was even listening to me. Hoping to get more movement out of her, I continued, "That was pretty good, Lex, but do you think you can you lift your right leg even higher?" And with that, she lifted her leg up so hard she flung it clear over the side of the bed, her eyes still closed. I dove to that side of the bed and put her leg back, glad that she had not fallen off the bed before I reached her. She always kept us smiling despite the seriousness of the situation.

By the end of the week, Lexi was not only able to wiggle her toes, lift her legs up, and stick out her tongue on command, but her therapists also got her out of bed and had her stand—albeit with a lot of assistance. Her legs were wobbly and awkward as she was helped to her feet. It took a great deal of effort for her to lock her knees in place so that she could stand up straight. With two physical therapists on either side, she took a couple steps forward. One therapist would slide Lexi's left foot forward, and then the other therapist would push her right foot. Her legs continued to buckle, but the therapists managed to hold her steady, keeping a firm grip on her arms, legs, and torso.

After walking like this for a few feet, Lexi was asked if she wanted to go back to bed, but she pointed forward, indicating that she wanted to keep practicing. Her determination showed on her face. These five-minute exercises would wear her out for the rest of the day, so we knew it was going to be a long and painful process for her to regain her abilities. But she was willing to "submit [herself] therefore to God" (James 4:7) and to all the afflictions that had come her way.

At one point, to break things up a bit, Cassidy asked Lexi if she wanted to have a thumb war. Cassidy begin singing and moving her thumb back and forth. The instant she did this, Lexi started to play, wiggling her thumb back and forth, and then, unexpectedly, she smashed Cassidy's thumb down so fiercely that Cassidy couldn't get out of her strong grip. Lexi was surging back to her former self with renewed vigor.

Fortunately, there was respite on occasion from the rigors of hospital life. On Wednesday, a week after the accident, one of my children allowed my good friend to come into the ICU just outside Lexi's room so I could say hi to her. We exchanged embraces, visited a little bit, and then I allowed her to come inside to see Lexi for a brief moment.

> The Lord is good, a strong hold in the day of trouble; and he knoweth them that trust in him.
> —Nahum 1:7

Just as she stepped through the doorway, Lexi's speech therapist entered and asked me who my guest was. For thirty years, I have referred to her as my sister, since most people have assumed we are because she looks so much like me. I told the therapist that she was my sister, partly out of habit and also because I didn't want to get in trouble for having someone in her room that was not a family member.

The therapist walked over to Lexi to start her therapy, and the first question she asked as she pointed to my friend was, "Is that your aunt?"

Luckily, Lexi couldn't talk, but she shook her head in a definite "No." My two other daughters in the room and I tried not to giggle. My friend averted the nurse's eyes and promptly slipped from the room while I distracted the therapist. The therapist thought Lexi's memory wasn't good, but we knew better.

Lexi was courageous during this week of hardship and

challenges. Her tenacity caused me to marvel. Her hope never faltered or melted away. Tears sprang to my eyes as I sat by her side, minute after minute, hour after hour, seeing firsthand that nothing could mask the throbbing pain she was called to bear. I, too, needed courage. I would not allow myself to ever feel distant from God's promises to Lexi. And deep within, I knew that I could continue to press on with courage because I was now solidly anchored in my faith and *could not* be moved.

Chapter Seventeen

THE MIRACLE OF REPENTANCE

And though the Lord give you the bread of adversity, and the water of affliction, yet shall not thy teachers be removed into a corner any more, but thine eyes shall see thy teachers: And thine ears shall hear a word behind thee, saying, This is the way, walk ye in it, when ye turn to the right hand, and when ye turn to the left.

—Isaiah 30:20–21

While spending countless hours in the hospital, we soon realized we were in a school of spiritual learning and that, unbeknownst to us, we still had a few more important lessons that we needed to learn.

On Friday morning, March 7, I was told by the doctor that if there was space available and if Lexi was doing well enough, she would be moved to the IMC Neuro Rehab Unit in Murray, Utah, later that afternoon. The doctor had notified me of this possibility a few days prior, but I had doubted it would happen anytime soon, as Lexi was in such poor condition. I also felt she needed to stay in the ICU a little longer. Although I had my misgivings, I was overjoyed at the possibility of her being transferred because I knew it meant she was progressing and would be coming home sooner.

That afternoon, the head of the clinic at IMC met with me and said Lexi qualified to go. Within a few minutes, we were packing up her few belongings, and she was loaded onto a gurney and taken in an ambulance to Murray, which is about forty-five minutes away, while I followed behind in my car. After arriving at the hospital in Murray, I found that the rehabilitation unit had many benefits that the ICU did not have. For example, Lexi was not limited to the rules of the ICU and could have any amount of family with her in her room at the same time. She could have friends visit her occasionally as well. Another benefit was that Lexi had a CNA assigned to be with her at all times to ensure she would never be alone. This meant we did not have to worry about having a family member with her at night. The following day, Saturday morning, the rehab staff started physical therapy with Lexi. My daughters offered to go to the hospital so I could spend time with my grandchildren before they had to return to their homes out of state. It was all I could do to not go to the hospital, and by 9 a.m., I knew I could not stay away from Lexi any longer. I left the kids with Parker.

As I walked into the rehab gym, I saw Lexi grab hold of two railings on either side of her and pull herself out of her wheelchair to a standing position. But as she did so, she cried out in excruciating pain and sat back down. Very concerned, I ran across the room to see what was wrong. However, the physical therapist explained that her brain signals were not working correctly, which meant that she thought she was in pain when she really wasn't. They further explained that her response was a completely normal reaction for a person with a traumatic brain injury.

I told them that I didn't believe that it was her brain playing tricks on her but that she was truly in pain. But because I didn't accept their theory, they asked me if I'd read the information booklet discussing brain injuries. I told them I hadn't, and they told me it was essential that I did. One of the therapists immediately left to get me a copy. When he returned, I took the book but didn't read it because I knew the pain she was experiencing was real and not a result of her brain injury.

I allowed them to have Lexi try to stand one more time. Again, she cried out in agony and sat back down. At this point in her recovery, Lexi was not able to speak much, so she wasn't able to describe the intensity of the pain or where it was coming from, yet the sound of her scream and the terrified grimace on her face said it all. I shuddered to see her in so much pain and was upset that I had allowed them to have her stand again.

I told the therapists that she wouldn't scream, especially with such intensity, unless she was experiencing real pain. I went on to insist that her leg be X-rayed, as I felt impressed that her leg was causing the pain. I

> He only is my rock and my salvation: he is my defence; I shall not be moved.
> —Psalm 62:6

also knew Lexi's unconquerable spirit and felt if she weren't in pain, she would be doing all she could to learn to stand again. I felt God guiding my steps through the Holy Ghost about what I should do.

Before they took her for the exam, they tried to talk me out of it, reminding me it was Saturday and, as such, I was inconveniencing a lot of people needlessly. They were certain it would be a waste of the doctor's time and my resources, but I wouldn't back down. Although annoyed at my demands, they granted my request, and Lexi was taken down to the radiology department for an X-ray.

When the results of the X-ray came back, they verified that Lexi had indeed suffered an injury to her leg. She had split her tibia in half, likely by hitting the side of the car during the accident. This explained why she was screaming in so much distress.

Later that day, the physician came to Lexi's room to explain the two options he had for fixing her leg. The first option included placing a thigh-high hard cast onto her leg that she would need to wear for eight weeks. The second choice included doing surgery to place a metal rod in her leg. Doing surgery would mean that she could be up and walking on her leg soon after the operation. If she had the hard cast, she would not be able to walk on it for eight weeks.

After explaining these options, the doctor stated he was certain surgery would be the best solution. I was worried for her to go into surgery for several reasons: she still required oxygen, I was afraid she would have to be intubated again and put back into the ICU after the operation, and I worried that she wouldn't wake up from the procedure. However, the doctor explained that Lexi wouldn't have to be put under anesthesia. She would be given a spinal block that would allow her to be awake during the procedure. After considering the possibilities and learning that the doctor was confident that surgery was the way to go, I followed his advice and scheduled it for the following morning.

Upon arriving at the hospital for the surgery in the chilly morning air, Doug and I were told it would take about an hour and then we would be able to see Lexi in recovery. However, after two hours had gone by with no word about how she was, I found myself starting to get concerned. After we had waited for almost three hours, we finally got a call from the surgeon telling us that the surgery had gone well and that the rod had been placed in her leg.

Following that phone call, the anesthesiologist came to inform us that although the plan was to do a spinal block for her surgery, he had been unable to get the needle into her spine. As a result, he had to put her under anesthesia, and she still had not woken up. The look on his face told me what I already knew inside.

I was devastated! From the beginning, I had my fears about Lexi being put under anesthesia, as I knew her lungs hadn't fully recovered from the accident. But despite my foreboding fears, all we could do was wait. I paced impatiently back and forth in the waiting room, endless questions marching through my mind. Each minute that passed chipped away at my peace. I took a calming breath and braced myself for the bad news as I picked up the phone and called the operating room to see if we could finally go back and see her.

There was a moment of silence on the other end. "Is this Lexi's mom?" a male voice asked.

"Yes. Why can't we come see Lexi?" I blurted out.

The doctor paused, and then hesitantly confided to me, "She is still having a difficult time breathing and needs to be monitored."

My shoulders fell and a heaviness settled in my chest. I took a deep breath and then released it, feeling a growing sense of uneasiness.

"What do you mean?" My voice held a sting. "Can't we at least be in the room with her?" I asked, puzzled and distressed.

> *Who comforteth [me] in all [my] tribulation.*
> —2 Corinthians 1:4

I didn't understand! Even when she was in a coma, we could be with her. I knew something was amiss, just as I had known about the injury to her leg the day prior. What had gone wrong? I felt stripped of my peace once again. My buried grief returned, lodging painfully in my heart. I struggled to regain my composure and to push my fear far from me.

"Is she . . . ?" Doug's voice trailed off as I nodded dejectedly, reading his thoughts as he sighed with disappointment.

As the day wore on and the minutes slowly ticked by, we grew more and more anxious to see her. Although I was extremely frustrated, I tried to be patient knowing God would "[comfort me] in all [my] tribulation" (2 Corinthians 1:4). But no answers were forthcoming.

After all she'd been through, I wondered how this could happen. Yet somehow I felt it was our family's fault that she was not doing well. This is because there had been some arguments on Friday and Saturday before the surgery, which had gravely bothered me. A few of our family members were mildly upset after debating about the number of visitors that should be allowed to visit Lexi and whether their children were being watched over properly while they were at the hospital. I believe our family's conflict had negatively affected Lexi, similar to when "Paul and Barnabas had no small dissension and disputation" (Acts 15:2).

Besides the disunity, I also knew that our prayers had become more casual as Lexi started to improve. When the accident first happened, we had stretched our souls by living a higher level of obedience and spirituality than we had ever before. Somehow, we had let ourselves relax and drift to a lower level of commitment as she progressed. The Spirit whispered to me that because the Lord had been the one to save Lexi, He could still take her back at any time if we did not always remember our complete dependence on Him. In other words, God would "prove [us], whether [we would] keep the way of the Lord to walk therein . . . or not" (Judges 2:22).

I started to plead to the Lord for forgiveness. I was sorry for not living up to what He expected of me and for anything I had done that might have caused her to return to the ICU. In my prayer, I "entered into a covenant to seek the Lord God . . . with *all* [my] heart and with *all* [my] soul"

> Be sober, be vigilant; because your adversary the devil, as a roaring lion, walketh about, seeking whom he may devour.
>
> —1 Peter 5:8

(2 Chronicles 15:12; italics added). I prayed to hear what I needed to hear and to do what I needed to do.

Finally, after the many hours of waiting, I heard the doctor call my name, and I whirled around to face the inevitable. He informed us that Lexi had been admitted to the Neuro Shock ICU, where she had been intubated again. And due to the surgery and pneumonia, she was struggling to breathe on her own. They had put on very high ventilator settings (seventy percent oxygen), which was the most breathing assistance she had ever needed.

The doctors did nearly every test possible to find out why she was struggling to breathe. They assumed that it was a pulmonary embolism, which is when a blood clot blocks one or more of the arteries to the lungs, obstructing the airway. Yet the tests didn't show that as the reason why she was not able to breathe on her own.

It was horrible and disappointing to see Lexi unconscious and back in the ICU, yet I knew that God was in charge of her future. If we wanted Heavenly Father to continue to be with Lexi, then we would have to show it—not only through our faith but also through our works.

That evening, Tanner came to the hospital and offered to pray over her. As Tanner placed his hands on her head, he paused mid-sentence and couldn't go on. As I listened to him struggle for words, my heart sank. A deafening silence descended upon the room. I knew how spiritual Tanner was and how powerful his past prayers had been, and my heart clutched with fear. I realized that what I had felt throughout

> [These] things doth the Lord hate; . . . he that soweth discord among brethren.
>
> —Proverbs 6:16, 19

the day was coming true—that Lexi might not be healed. As Tanner continued to pause, I began to pray with greater fervency for our Father in Heaven to heal her, and I pondered if the Lord would allow Lexi to continue to be with us. I chided myself for anything I might have said or done to cause the rift between us and God's healing power to Lexi. Finally, after what seemed like an eternity, the words came to Tanner, and he was able to continue. I breathed an audible sigh of relief.

Afterward, he told us that he was being rebuked by the Lord for our entire family. He explained that we had been too relaxed in our pleadings on behalf of Lexi to the Lord. We had just *expected* the miracle to continue on without being grateful to Him and acknowledging *His* hand in it all.

I had not said anything to Tanner about my concerns before, yet the Spirit told us both individually that Heavenly Father was not pleased with us for forgetting to rely on Him more fully during Lexi's recovery. Lowering my voice to a whisper, I told Tanner that I had known all day that the Lord was not happy with our family for not being exactly obedient and that it was the cause for the delay in Lexi's progress. We had not been fixed on God's purpose in order to have the heavens opened to us. I knew from the beginning of her accident that we couldn't engage in conflict because of the enormous price we would pay in driving the Spirit away as well as the angels that were attending to her. We prayed for forgiveness and committed to do better. And soon a radiance welled up inside me, and I knew we had been forgiven.

Although we felt an immeasurable sense of reprieve that Lexi had once again been spared, we were weary and spent.

By the time Doug and I headed home, the air outside had turned cool, and dusk had already settled over the city. The once busy streets were seemingly empty when we got into our car. Although I was sad because of another setback, relief surged through me. I knew that each step of the way we had been blessed with sensitive hearts and inspired minds to give us what we needed. We would "hope continually" (Psalm 71:14). We would "go in the strength of the Lord" (Psalm 71:16) so that the Lord would "incline [His] ear unto [us]" (Psalm 71:2).

Because of the trials Lexi had just gone through and the fact that she was back in the ICU again, my daughter Shelby suggested that we start a continuous fast for her. Each day of the week, a member of our family would fast so that every day someone would be fasting for her. Individually, we felt that we needed to show the Lord we were serious about our commitment to call down His power from heaven to heal Lexi both mentally and physically. Through every setback, trial, and heartache our family experienced, we were able to say with absolute clarity, "The Lord is my light and my salvation; whom shall I fear? the Lord is the strength of my life; of whom shall I be afraid? . . . Wait on the Lord: be of good courage, and he shall strengthen thine heart: wait, I say, on the Lord" (Psalm 27:1, 14).

God did indeed hear our prayers of repentance and thanksgiving, because the next day, Lexi was extubated, although she continued to need the ventilator. We had learned a very valuable lesson that would stay with us the rest of our lives. It was a clear reminder that our actions do indeed determine how much the powers of heaven can be distilled upon us and our loved ones. The earlier pain and darkness I had experienced transformed into joy and light. It flowed through me and penetrated my heart.

Chapter Eighteen

THE MIRACLE OF THE WHISPERINGS OF THE SPIRIT

Hast thou not known? hast thou not heard, that the everlasting God, the Lord, the Creator of the ends of the earth, fainteth not, neither is weary? there is no searching of his understanding.

—Isaiah 40:28

On the first day we arrived at the rehab center—before we had discovered her broken leg—the doctor asked Lexi who I was in order to assess her memory. Up to this point in her recovery, she had always answered that question correctly. But on this day, she looked at me and said, without hesitation, in a voice slightly slurred and lifeless, "Michael Jackson."

My eyes widened, and a chill shot through me. The doctor then pointed to my daughter Shelby and asked who she was, and Lexi said feebly, "A rock star," her face expressionless.

With a look of horror, I glanced at Shelby. From the moment Lexi had come out of the coma, her brain and memory had seemed to be intact, so I couldn't understand why she would answer this way now. At first, I thought she might have been teasing us with her comical answers and waited for her to giggle, but she didn't.

The rehab doctor informed us that her bizarre answers were totally normal for someone with a brain injury. But to me, her answers were very worrisome. However, I knew things would be okay in the long run because of the blessings she had been given that said she'd make a full recovery, so I brushed aside my concern.

> But the Spirit itself maketh intercession for us.
>
> —Romans 8:26

I didn't have much time to think about her odd behavior because the very next day was the day we learned that her tibia had been broken, which resulted in her returning to the ICU. All our thoughts and prayers were then focused on her regaining the ability to breathe on her own again.

But a few days after she was stabilized in the ICU, Lexi was muttering some phrases that didn't make sense. My heart was troubled. This time, the Spirit whispered to me that it wasn't her head injury that was causing her to say these outlandish comments. I immediately jumped up from my chair to find a nurse and asked her to check the medications that Lexi was on and what the side effects were. Sure enough, one of the side effects of her medications caused hallucinations. I told the nurse to take her off that drug immediately.

Almost daily I felt guided by God in Lexi's behalf, as thoughts would come into my mind to know how to help Lexi. I can attribute this in a large part to a blessing my son-in-law Daniel had offered a few days after the accident. He promised me that in every instance, I would be inspired and prompted to know exactly what to do to facilitate Lexi's healing. In every way and through every experience, I could see that the blessing he gave me was being fulfilled, for "all that the Lord hath spoken [would I] do," (Exodus 19:8) and "what the Lord saith [would] I speak." (1 Kings 22:14). I was relying on inspiration, not knowledge, and that made all the difference.

When Lexi's doctor came to check up on her, I asked him why he had given that particular drug to Lexi. He told me that he was just continuing to administer the same medicine the doctors from the previous hospital had prescribed for her. He continued to explain to me that those pills were usually given to treat Alzheimer patients but that occasionally some doctors used them for patients with severe brain injuries to help their memory.

I was not happy when I heard this, since her mind had been good from the moment she awoke from her coma. I felt they were using Lexi as a guinea pig, and the medicine was making her thought patterns worse. It came as a great relief to have the doctor agree with me. He wrote on her chart that she was allergic to that particular drug so she would not be given it again.

It took a week or more for that medication to wear off. In the meantime, her conversations continued to be a little odd. She alternated regularly between fantasy and reality. One of the side effects of the medication caused her to be obsessed with the piano. Everything she mentioned had the word *piano* in it. She would say with considerable anxiety on her face, "I want to wear my piano pants. They are over there in my piano drawer," or "I can't go for a walk because I need to practice the piano." Disappointment crossed her face when I told her the hospital didn't have a piano.

One afternoon, she begged me to let her have the phone to text her friends to thank them for a sweet note they'd written her, but instead of thanking them for the letter, she thanked them for their beautiful piano concerto. Still another day, her eyes shining with hope, she muttered, "Is that popcorn over there?" pointing toward the sink in her room.

Let a double portion of thy spirit be upon me.

—2 Kings 2:9

I looked at her without even a small hint of amusement, "Nope." A shiver ran through me when I thought of her nonsensical talk.

"Are you sure?" Her voice was soft. She let out a sigh, and her shoulders slumped slightly. She was determined there was popcorn everywhere and wanted some desperately.

Other times, she seemed distraught and puzzled when we would try to get her to do therapy, believing instead that she should be at school.

"I'm late, I have a class right now," she would say obviously agitated. "I'm going to fail my classes, so I can't do therapy." She seemed stressed and worried.

I felt more than just a twinge of concern and swallowed my nervousness. I would remind her that she was in the hospital because she had been hit by a car and that her teachers knew about the accident, so she didn't need to worry. Luckily, my words usually worked, and she understood what was happening around her.

One morning, just like every other morning, I walked in and kissed her on the cheek. She usually smiled when I did this, but on that day, because of the medicine she was on, she scowled at me and growled, "Why do you keep doing that?" Her voice still low and reserved.

"Because I love you," I responded.

"Well, it's not fair."

"What's not fair?"

"I can't love you back!" she mumbled in quiet frustration. I suppressed a smile at her innocent response. Even though she was confused, she still felt guilty that she was a taker and not a giver.

On other occasions, she would forget family member's names even though she had previously remembered their name from the beginning of her recovery. One day, my daughter Kelsi came to visit Lexi on her lunch break. Testing Lexi's memory, I pointed to Kelsi when she walked in the room and asked, "What's her name?"

Lexi looked at her with a blank stare. "I don't remember," her voice strained in a whisper. Her shoulders lifted, then fell in disappointment.

I was surprised that she couldn't remember, so to help jog her memory, I asked her questions about our home.

"Do you remember that we have chickens at home?"

She responded in the affirmative. "What are their names?" I asked.

Without hesitation she said, "Daisy, Ace, and Dixie."

Kelsi immediately blurted out, "You remember the chicken's names, but you don't remember my name?"

Thinking that she would remember her sister's name now, I pointed to Kelsi again and asked, "So what's her name?"

She gave Kelsi a quizzical look, and then as if suddenly remembering, she blurted out, "Daisy?" I struggled to maintain a straight face.

Lexi's face twisted into a knitted brow. "I know who you are. I just can't think of your name right now." Her voice trailed off in regret. It was frustrating for her not to remember.

The very next day Tanner came to visit Lexi. He often made the forty-five-minute trip on TRAX, the commuter train, by himself or with his wife, Mandy, to visit Lexi. He had taken a lot of time away from his schooling at the beginning of the accident, and he was worried he would not pass his classes at BYU. But Lexi was his first priority, and he continued to make the trips to be with her, giving up much-needed sleep to do so.

When visitors entered Lexi's room, as a normal routine, the nurses would quiz Lexi to facilitate her memory, and today was no exception. "Who is this guy?" the nurse asked.

Lexi blurted out without the smallest hint of a grin, "My boyfriend."

Tanner and I stood there in stunned silence. Was her memory that bad? But quick as a wink, she grinned sheepishly, "Just kidding. He's my brother."

Tanner tipped back his head and laughed hysterically. Unbeknownst to us, Lexi had been listening to our concerns about her memory since the surgery and decided to play a trick on us. I was relieved and laughed for days about how she had managed to tease us. She had given us a needed distraction from the mundane hospital life. And it was also a good indication of how sharp her mind was.

When Lexi could start comprehending things more clearly toward the end of the week, I asked her, "Do you remember how you had talked about being a motivational speaker for the last couple of years?"

Lexi had decided in high school that she wanted to be a motivational speaker and would talk to me quite often about her career choice. Speaking in public wasn't easy for her, but she was determined to become a polished orator. She was excited for her first public speaking class in college. It came as a surprise then when she came home one weekend and exclaimed, "Mom, I need a new major!"

I stopped what I was doing and turned around to face her. "What? Why is that?" I inquired. She was not one to change majors on a whim. When she had a goal, she stuck with it. I was perplexed by her statement.

"I can't be a motivational speaker anymore," she said.

"Why would you say that?" I asked, genuinely surprised.

"It just dawned on me that every motivational speaker has a bad accident," she said, shrugging her shoulders. "So yeah, can't be one now." Her smile had long since faded, and the sparkle had left her eyes. She had convinced herself that her long-held dream was no longer a possibility.

Remembering that conversation, Lexi rolled her eyes and shook her head as if to say, "Oh man, I really jinxed myself, didn't I?"

> He that hath an ear, let him hear what the Spirit saith.
> —Revelations 3:6

God had a plan for Lexi—as he does for each of us— and it was exhilarating to have a front row seat and see the events of her life unfold. I couldn't help but marvel, especially when I reflected on how the Lord was directing me through the whisperings of the Spirit to know the best way to help her recover.

Chapter Nineteen

THE MIRACLE
OF PATIENCE

*And to stand every morning to thank and praise the Lord,
and likewise at even.*

—1 Chronicles 23:30

We were extremely excited the following Wednesday when Lexi left the ICU—for the second time—and went back upstairs to the rehab center. When she left, they gave her a small respiratory mask that formed a mist. When inhaled, it helped her with her breathing difficulties. I was concerned about those difficulties. Then much to our dismay, within a couple hours, she was back down in the ICU again.

Doug had arrived late in the evening to be with Lexi until she fell asleep for the night, so I left to go home. Before I left, I gave strict instructions to both him and the nurse that Lexi was not to have more medicine than the dosage she was allotted. I repeated these instructions several times. For some reason, I was worried she would be given too much.

He was a little annoyed with me for my repeated instructions, thinking I didn't trust him, but I just had a foreboding feeling about her receiving too much medication that night. I almost didn't leave the hospital because of it. Within a half hour after I left, the nurse gave Lexi her medication. About that time, Lexi had some visitors that stayed for about ten minutes or so.

After they left, Doug and the nurse were sitting with Lexi, when the nurse got a startled look on her face and asked, "Does Lexi look gray to you?"

Doug jumped up and tried to wake Lexi. She was unresponsive. He shook her arms and nudged her, trying to wake her up, but she didn't respond. He started to panic and yelled at the nurse to get someone right away. Within what seemed like a minute, there were fifteen people in her room working frantically to revive her. Code red over the intercom really brings hospital staff from everywhere!

Soon after, he called me to tell me what was happening. I shot up from my chair, my tired limbs completely forgotten. My mind was racing; my stomach tightened in fear. "What happened? Is she all right?" My words chocked in my throat. "Is she breathing?" My heart was thumping wildly in my chest searching for answers. I was drowning in grief, hardly believing that this could be happening again. Less than an hour before, she had been happy and talking. In the back of my mind, I wondered how I could possibly survive another heart-wrenching ordeal.

Tears spilled down my cheeks, my knees gave way, and I collapsed on the floor. I couldn't wrap my mind around what had just happened.

My daughter Cassidy, seeing my condition, went next door to ask our neighbor, who is also her father-in-law, if he would come pray over me for a blessing of comfort and peace. As he placed his hands on my head, my crying subsided and my eyes no longer burned. I felt a strong feeling of comfort come over me, and I knew she would be okay as the importance of his words sunk deep. The Savior was there again for me. I was learning first-hand how He was indeed sent to "heal the brokenhearted" (Luke 4:18). And this time, I was reassured her condition had nothing to do with our family's righteousness.

Sensing how devastated I was, Doug called me back and told me I didn't need to return to the hospital because Lexi had stabilized and everything was fine. He didn't let me know that she still hadn't regained consciousness.

Strengthened with all might, according to his glorious power, unto all patience and longsuffering with joyfulness; giving thanks unto the Father, which hath made us meet to be partakers of the inheritance of the saints in light.

—Colossians 1:11–12

We learned several days later that the pharmacist had written a prescription for three times the amount of medication that Lexi was supposed to be given, which is why she had stopped breathing. We were grateful that the Spirit let us know immediately that this setback was not because of something we had done or failed to do. But it was a reminder to me that even though we might be doing our best to pray and focus on the Savior, bad things still happen.

It was terrifying to think how close we came to losing Lexi that night. The Lord may have wept seeing us in such turmoil of spirit as He does for all those who suffer similar trials. The scriptures teach us about this aspect of the Savior's divine nature: "And it came to pass that the God of heaven looked upon the residue of the people, and he wept" (Moses 7:28). He loves us and cares deeply for us and wants to help us bear the trials that come upon us here in mortality.

> We glory in tribulations also: knowing that tribulation worketh patience; and patience, experience; and experience, hope.
>
> —Romans 5:3–4

Although we were extremely grateful that Lexi was alive, we were discouraged that she had to be intubated again, as this set her back quite a few steps in her recovery. The Apostle Paul's words couldn't have been more poignant to us: "[We had] need of patience . . . after [we had] done the will of God" (Hebrews 10:36). As we waited for Lexi's body to heal, we were being taught that "tribulation worketh patience" (Romans 5:3). I was allowed to internalize the omnipotence of the Savior more completely through this type of suffering. As described in Isaiah, "For a small moment [I felt] forsaken. . . . But with everlasting kindness

[I was given] mercy" (Isaiah 54:7–8). I continued to experience for myself that coming to Christ and allowing Him to carry my load was the only way to peace.

Chapter Twenty

THE MIRACLE OF BEING FILLED WITH LIGHT

And the sheep follow him: for they know his voice.

—John 10:4

At five o'clock the next morning, I returned to the hospital, determined that there would not be another setback in Lexi's recovery. I was devastated that she was back in the ICU unit—intubated and hooked up with a catheter—for the third time. It seemed that each time she began to make a small amount of progress, something unforeseen would happen, resulting in her having to regain her faculties over again. But I needed to remember the command, "Be thou strong and very courageous" (Joshua 1:7).

It was around 7 a.m. when Lexi's trauma doctor made his rounds to her room. Having been informed of my concerns and knowing this was our third time in the ICU, he was genuinely sympathetic and invited me to write a list of issues that I felt needed to be addressed. He said they would distribute it to the staff to use as a guideline. His invitation startled me, and I was touched to see understanding in his eyes. It was refreshing to have a doctor of his prestige who was humble enough to ask for my opinion and suggestions and then follow them, instead of insisting that because of his superior knowledge with trauma patients, he should be the sole expert. His face was kind and gentle. Each day, he had me brief him on what I felt her needs were and how I thought they could best help her. In just a few short days, he taught me about compassion, humility, and the gift of listening. The head nurse also went the extra mile, giving me her personal phone number to call when she was not at the hospital. I was touched by their genuine interest in Lexi's well-being.

One request I made was for Lexi be given more time with her therapist. They quickly obliged, starting Lexi on the long process of learning to walk again. She had two physical therapists take her a few hundred yards down the hall and back, her oxygen tank in tow. Sometimes, she couldn't make it down the hall, and they would grab a chair for her until she gained enough strength to return to the room.

When she went on these exceedingly short walks, I found it amusing that she would immediately head to the drinking fountain. It was always a huge disappointment to her when she was told she couldn't have any water. Eventually, she was allowed to get a small one-inch sponge attached to a stick to dip in water. The joy she expressed in getting a few drops of water is etched in my memory, and it will always make me happy to think of it. As she dipped the sponge in the water, she would beam and

> *That they might have my joy fulfilled in themselves.*
>
> —John 17:13

exclaim, "Yummy!" A tiny smile would light up her eyes. Each time she tasted the water, she would say the same thing over and over with as much fervor and joy as she could muster. Her face was a picture of pure delight.

She was still enjoying her drops of water the second day after she returned to the ICU when her two-year-old nephew Calvin came to visit. He observed her delight as she squeezed the water out of the sponge into her mouth. Of course seeing her enjoyment, he wanted what she was having. So I got a cup of water and sponge for him and sat him in the bed next to her. I thought for sure he would be disappointed when he tasted it and found out it was just water. Much to our surprise, he was just as thrilled as Lexi. They would both squeal in delight chanting, "Yummy! Yummy!" and look at each other and giggle. It was as if they had just raided the candy store and were relishing their tasty morsels. A smile stole across my face, feeling their joy. Moments like this, when we could laugh, helped ease our burden. We found humor was a gift and we cherished any time we could enjoy playful encounters with one another.

> *Be careful for nothing; but in every thing by prayer and supplication with thanksgiving let your requests be made known unto God. . . . For I have learned, in whatsoever state I am, therewith to be content. I know both how to be abased, and I know how to abound: every where and in all things I am instructed both to be full and to be hungry, both to abound and to suffer need.*
>
> —Philippians 4:6, 11–12

After a few days, Lexi was strong enough to leave the ICU and return to the rehab floor. I was wary of her going back since the previous two times she had returned to the rehab center, it had taken less than a day to get readmitted to the ICU. Luckily for Lexi, her progress went uphill from that moment on with only a few minor complications.

Early in the morning, on her second day back in the rehab center, I was standing talking to Lexi's doctor when I heard Lexi weakly mutter, "Thanks." Out of the corner of my eye, I saw that a technician who had come to check the equipment in the room was just leaving, and Lexi was acknowledging him for his service. A few minutes later, as I continued my discussion with the doctor, a cleaning lady came in the room and took out the garbage. Again, I heard a barely audible "thank you" from Lexi. Since her room was always a revolving door of visitors, it wasn't long before a nurse appeared in the room to check her vitals, and once again, there was a raspy, unclear "thanks" coming from her lips.

This time, I stopped talking and turned to look over at Lexi. I was dumbfounded. Here she was, lying in a hospital bed with a neck brace that made it virtually impossible to move her head. Her throat was sore and tender from having the breathing tube taken in and out over the last several weeks. Plus, she had a feeding tube in her nose. Her head hurt so much that she would cry out in agony every few hours, begging for more pain medication to ease the pounding in her head. She wouldn't even allow me to touch her hair because of how tender her scalp was. Yet there she was, showing gratitude to people left and right as they came into her room to perform their normal everyday duties.

I continued to observe her the rest of the day. I noticed that she never stopped showing her appreciation, even when they asked her to do something she detested, like making her blow puffs of air into her oxygen device. She was always sincere, her eyes shining with goodness. I had to chuckle under my breath when the nurse came back with a syringe and slid the needle into her forearm. With teeth clenched, Lexi still managed to whisper a quiet "thank you" as she grimaced in discomfort.

I think I heard her say thank you at least thirty times a day. She had every excuse not to be thankful and to resent the fact she couldn't eat, walk, or swallow; yet, she had a spirit of gratitude. I knew I needed to remember this experience. I wanted this mental picture indelibly etched in my mind.

I lay down next to her, put my legs inside her blankets, and gently took her hand as I laid my head on her shoulder and closed my eyes. I just wanted to be next to her, hoping that maybe some of her goodness would seep deep into my soul and change me for the better. She was so good and Christlike. The evening shadows began to emerge, darkening

Christ shall give thee light.
—Ephesians 5:14

177

her room, and stillness permeated our space. Although I could still hear the humming of the machines surrounding her bed, the place seemed suddenly still and peaceful. As I continued to nestle next to her, my heart swelled with thanksgiving for each and every day that she had been allowed to remain with us. Oh, how I loved her! Throughout her life, she had taught me by her example, and now she was teaching me again that true character is manifested by how we react when faced with adversity. As I had watched her throughout the day, I understood more completely how gratitude does indeed have the power to bring us happiness in the worst of circumstances.

Each day, I seemed to glean something from Lexi, and the next afternoon proved to be no exception. Tanner and I were visiting her, and she asked me in her still faint voice, "Can you tell me some stories that happened to me in the hospital? Because I have no memory of anything."

"Hmm, let's see . . ." my voice trailed off as I tried to think of a story I had not told her.

"Remember when she started kicking her leg after being so still?" Tanner said with a sly grin on his face.

I started to laugh as I rested my hand lightly on her arm. "Oh, yeah! You were still in a coma, but you started kicking your left leg up and down over and over again until you were almost off the bed. Mandy was standing at the foot of your bed at the time and gently moved your legs away from the side of the bed and tucked them under your sheet."

"That's nice of her," Lexi chimed in.

"Yes, it was nice of her because you were getting really close to the edge of the bed with that kicking motion. But just as she got your feet situated, you picked up your leg again and kicked her in the stomach!"

"Yeah," Tanner snickered, "I had been watching this unfold across the room, and I was thinking to myself, 'Holy cow, she is one determined girl. She's letting us know—even in a coma—not to mess with her.' It was hilarious, Lex. We couldn't stop laughing."

Lexi's reaction to the story was priceless. She bemoaned, "Why would I do that? Did I tell her I was sorry?"

I tried hard not to smile at her sweet, innocent response and leaned down to stroke her hair. I caught her eye and winked at her, "No, Lexi, you were in a coma, but that is so kind of you to care about her feelings. I'm sure she understood."

Lexi was truly filled with light.

Chapter Twenty-One

THE MIRACLE OF FACING TOWARD THE SON

Confirming the souls of the disciples, and exhorting them to continue in the faith, and that we must through much tribulation enter into the kingdom of God.

—Acts 14:22

On the night of her accident, three of Lexi's good friends wanted to do something for her. They decided to set up a page on Facebook called "Pray for Lexi." It was a brilliant idea. The page was shared by hundreds of people from all over the world. As the news converged on the Internet, it garnered well over thirty-two thousand followers in less than a week, with some posts exceeding three hundred thousand views.

It was a great blessing to Lexi to have so many people praying and fasting for her. Our family took over managing the page the day after the accident, because it was the fastest and most convenient way to give updates on her condition. Kelsi wrote each post from the information I provided her for the first two weeks, and then I took over managing it completely until Lexi was able to do so herself several months later. It's clear that Lexi's friends were inspired to set up this page after reading how Lexi's story affected so many people for good.

A common thread came from those we had never met but prayed for her nonetheless: "I don't know you or your family, but I want you to know your story has touched my life. I fasted for Lexi and your family today. Miracles happen!"

Another poster wrote, "This is so beautiful. I will keep praying for this darling girl who I don't even know and have never met. I know all these prayers from all these wonderful people are helping this sweet girl. God is a God of miracles! We have all witnessed one with your post today. Thank you for sharing . . . heaven's help was near."

We also received a message from a lady who told us that as she was shopping on Saturday, the day before the fast, the sweetest little girl handed her a flyer with Lexi's story and the title "Pray for Lexi" on it. Our neighbor Todd had created and distributed thousands of these flyers, with the help of neighbors, to get the word out. She thought it was touching and wrote, "Of course, I have kept her in my prayers. That little girl who handed the flyer to me was so precious. I thought how important it is for each of us to 'bear one another's burdens.'"

We were so grateful for these acts of kindness and compassion. And not only was Lexi blessed because of those who fasted and prayed for her, but there were countless others whose hearts were softened and inspired to believe in God again. For example, this was a note that came to my daughter:

Hi Kelsi, It's [name removed] from high school. I am sure you have had many messages come through about your sister.

But I felt like I really needed to tell you—and maybe your sister one day how deeply touched I am by her story. I've also read your sister-in-law Mandy's blog post, and I have been following "Pray for Lexi"!

Anyways, I have been struggling with knowing if God was real and if He knew me since September of last year, give or take. It hasn't been easy, and at times, I wonder why I am wasting my time. Recently, the past month about, I have been praying to understand why I feel the way I do. I was raised in a great God-fearing home. My husband has a strong belief in God, but he wasn't going to push something on me. . . . He wanted me to figure it out on my own. I was invited to follow "Pray for Lexi." Reading the posts and seeing the faith your sweet family has and the love you have for the gospel has truly touched me. I owe it to Lexi and your family for helping me realize what was right and what I needed in my life. Thank you! Thank you! Thank you! You and your family are so amazing! I will keep you in my prayers.

And there are even more examples of the dramatic change that was occurring in the lives of many:

I know my prayer for her last night was the first time I have prayed in months.

Mona explained,

You have touched me in so many ways and helped restore my faith in God just when I thought I'd lost it forever. You are a living angel. Bless you.

Becky wrote from far-away Africa of their new-found understanding of prayer:

The Bible says, "If Christ be for us, who can be against us?" Lexi, my friends and I in Ghana are praying for you, and I know it's just a matter of time until you will be up on your feet again. You're a very strong girl, and nothing can break you down, not even what the doctor says. . . . You're not just a fighter; you're a Victor. Your story has challenged me to the fact that no mountain is too high to prevent God's divine miracle from reaching us. Christ is bigger than whatever you're going through. You don't know how much strength people from all the ends of the world are pulling from your story. You're rising up again to be what you've always dreamed of becoming. Lots of love from Ghana, and, Lex, nothing is impossible for our Christ.

And a young twenty-year-old named Braxton, who was a Christian missionary, drew strength from the prayers for Lexi as well. He felt inspired to use her story when he was helping a young single mom and her son who were struggling not only physically to make ends meet but also spiritually. He knew that teaching her about the power of prayer is what she needed most at this time in her life. Braxton wrote,

> So last Monday, I felt pretty low. I wasn't too happy because I was thinking about what happened to Lexi Hansen. I was with a friend helping a lady who is twenty-seven and her son who is fourteen. As we were helping her, I happened to glance up and noticed that she had a paper on her fridge that talked about praying as a family. So the thought came to me to talk to her about prayer. As we shared a scripture, Lexi's story came to mind. As I shared the story of what had happened and how she had improved through the faith and prayer of so many people throughout the world, the story brought the Spirit into the room, and you could feel its presence. She felt it and by the end was completely speechless as the Spirit testified to her of the power of prayer. Ever since then, she has been praying morning and night and attended church for the second time in my five months here.

As I sat on the bed next to Lexi at the hospital, I began to read some of these messages people had written about her on

Facebook. I wanted her to know about all the people that she had influenced through her faith and courage.

"Look at the impact you have had on so many people," I said. "They are turning to God because of you."

Lexi started to tear up and asked, perplexed, "Why? Why would they say that?"

"Because they looked at your Facebook page to see what you had posted before the accident. A lot of these people didn't know you and wanted to see what type of person you were."

> *Who knoweth whether thou art come to the kingdom for such a time as this?*
>
> —Esther 4:14

"Yeah, but what did I do? I still don't get it." Her face softened in the gentle query.

"Well . . . it was apparent to them from reading your posts that you had tried to *always* walk in the light of the Lord, that God was most important to you."

A smile touched her eyes as if she were beginning to comprehend. "What did I write about? I don't remember much," she said.

"Remember each Sunday you would write inspiring messages about God and counsel them to follow his teachings?"

She couldn't hide her emotions as her lip began to quiver, tears of joy streaming down her face as she nestled her head on my shoulder. "Makes me so happy," she whispered reverently, a smile on her face.

I knew how much this meant to her because in her life, she had wanted to turn people to Christ.

Even though Lexi had helped and was helping many people turn to Christ, one day in particular stands out in my memory—the day it was Lexi's turn to need spiritual help. It was early

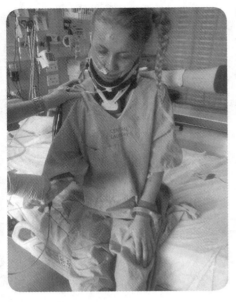

morning, and Lexi's occupational therapists had just come into her room to assist her to the gym, where they would work with her on cognitive skills. When I tried to get Lexi out of bed, she refused to get up and started to cry. She acted confused and distraught over the situation. I could tell that she didn't know where she was and, even more frightening, *who* she was. She threw her arms around me and sobbed in aching despair.

I tried to console her. "Lex, you are in the hospital. You had a bad accident and got hit by a car," I explained to her, but it didn't help. She continued to act irrationally. Her dark eyes clouded with uncertainty.

Suddenly I knew what to do to help her. I sprang instantly into action and ran over to a small table in the room and grabbed our family picture. In the meantime, Lexi had collapsed back down on the bed, so I knelt beside the bed and pushed the picture under her face and stared intently into her eyes and asked softly, "Lexi, do you see these people? Do you know who they are?"

She stared intently for a long moment, her eyes moving over each family member. Almost instantly she stopped crying, her eyes softening before nodding her head.

I placed my hands against her cheeks, and then, releasing one hand, I pointed to her in the family picture and inquired, "Do you know who this is?"

Again there was a pause as she studied the photo. Suddenly,

her eyes lit up, and she slowly nodded her head, a sense of recognition resting on her.

I excitedly responded, "Lexi, that's you. You are Lexi. This is your family." I could tell that her understanding of who she was and to whom she belonged had returned.

She wiped her tears with her sleeve, and her lips stopped quivering as she fought for composure. I then helped her sit up in bed, and we held each other tight as a few tears of joy escaped down her cheeks. It was a tender moment for the two of us. She knew who she was now, and a whisper of a smile touched her face. She was Lexi, a daughter of God, part of an earthly family who loved her, and that made all the difference. With that knowledge, there were no more tears and no more confusion. That is the message that she tried to portray on Facebook over the years that we are God's children and that He loves us.

> *looking unto Jesus the author and finisher of our faith.*
> —Hebrews 12:2

The knowledge that she was a child of God continued to burn bright as we wheeled Lexi to church services in the hospital a few days later. I don't remember anything that was said that Sunday, but I still have an image etched in my memory from that day.

The sacrament had been blessed and was being passed to the congregation. Lexi, so weak and frail, instinctively reached for it, forgetting for a minute she had a feeding tube and could not swallow without aspirating. I gently held back her hand and whispered to her that although she was not able to eat the bread, she could press it to her lips as a symbol of her desire to honor God's covenants. A forlorn look crept onto her face. For Lexi, this was not enough to show her love for God; she wanted to reveal her devotion to the Lord by total and complete obedience. Lowering her head dejectedly, she stared at her clasped hands while tears tumbled gently from her eyes and onto her lap.

Our family members also benefited from Lexi's spiritual sensitivity. Cassidy explains:

> Lexi, in my mind, has always been so childlike. Her countenance and demeanor reflect what Christ says in the scriptures to "become as little children" (Matthew 18:3). To a lot of people, Lexi may come across as naïve, but she's not. She acts according to what the Savior has taught to be submissive and meek like unto a child. Children are very quick to forgive and forget. They are filled with an immense amount of love for all those around them. Lexi is the same. She loves everybody she meets.
>
> When this accident happened to her, I knew right away it was because she had such an innocent and pure soul. She had an important role to fulfill, and the Lord knew He could trust her to achieve a change in the lives of countless individuals throughout the world. She saw the importance of this life, grasped it firmly, and worked hard to achieve a stronger testimony and foundation of what she knew to be true. Each time I visited home after getting married, when

Lexi answered the door, she did so with the biggest, brightest smile. An immediate chain reaction would take place, and I would be grinning from ear to ear. I couldn't help but think how beautiful life was. Lexi brought this spirit to everyone. She always gave me her full attention, listening to whatever I had to say and was always excited and proud of me. She had a way of bringing joy and hope to the world again.

I believe that the reason Lexi's countenance was almost always happy and filled with light is because she tried to always face toward the Son, God's Son.

Our ability to be of good cheer is in direct relation to how connected we are to Christ. Lexi stayed close to Christ, and as a result, could chase the darkness away when she entered a room because of the light of truth she had welcomed into her heart. Her life revealed her desire to face the Son.

Chapter Twenty-Two

THE MIRACLE OF WALKING WITH GOD

And I will walk among you, and will be your God, and ye shall be my people.

—Leviticus 26:12

At this point in Lexi's recovery, my days became repetitive and routine in nature. Each morning at five thirty, I showered, dressed, went downstairs to read scriptures, and said a family prayer with Parker, who was a senior in high school.

Doug left for work about the time I woke up. From the earliest days of our marriage, he had been an early riser and worked late into the night, even on Saturdays. But with Lexi in the hospital, he gladly adjusted his schedule to stay with her during the evening hours. I was grateful for this so I could get home before Parker went to bed and have family prayer together.

I didn't like leaving the house before Parker left for school, nor did I like having him come home to an empty house, but I had no other choice. That's why the sliver of time together with him in the morning and in the evening was so important to me. After our prayer, I gave Parker a hug and a kiss and hurried out the door to get to the hospital before the doctors made their rounds. More importantly, I wanted to be there before Lexi woke up.

Once I got to the hospital, it was actually refreshing to have a change of pace, an opportunity to have even more time to ponder, to read God's word, and to become better in tune with the Spirit. I sat by Lexi's window to catch the first morning rays on my open book, glancing periodically over at her. I didn't want to waste time wishing for her recovery to pass. Instead, I wanted to find out what I should learn from each experience. Her challenges would refine my character as well. The more I tried to be connected to the Savior each day, the happier I became.

> *Walk in the light, as he is in the light.*
>
> —1 John 1:7

One morning, I had been there for about an hour before I heard the rustle of sheets and some moaning. I quickly got up, took her hand and kissed it.

"Good morning, Lexi." I smiled wide, hoping to bring some sunshine to her trials.

> *Though I walk in the midst of trouble, thou wilt revive me: thou shalt stretch forth thine hand.*
>
> —Psalm 138:7

Opening her eyes, I could tell she was in pain. "I need pills," she groaned; the words were slurred.

I swept a lock of her hair back so I could see her eyes and she instantly recoiled. I forgot that touching her hair was off limits. I knew instantly from seeing her pain-stricken eyes, before she had uttered a word, that I needed to call for a nurse to get her medicine, but the nurse was delayed.

When Lexi begged me to get the nurse again, her pain was so intense that I couldn't sit still. The pleading in her voice was forceful. I rushed out of the room without hesitation, searching the nurses' station and halls, but the place was deserted. Other patients were being attended to. My emotions rose to the surface, and I pursed my lips hard, swallowing back the tears to stay in control. I hated watching her suffer more than anything else. Lexi, on the other hand, couldn't hold back the tears, and they trickled down her cheeks, spilling onto her pillow.

I was grateful her therapy started early because it was a good distraction from her grievous pain. I tried to help her dress, but she groaned, "I'm dressed," pointing to the basketball shorts and a T-shirt she had worn to bed. "I want to wear this," her voice trailed off.

It was obvious the throbbing in her head that lingered every minute, every second of the day, was just too much. I was sympathetic to her plight, knowing how it added to her pain and would wear her out just by changing her clothes. Her voice exhaled in relief as she peered up at me with barely a half smile, all that she could muster.

Watching her had opened my eyes to suffering, I had never seen before, and that image lay heavily before me. Suffering manifested itself in her every movement. I realized there would be more soul stretching in the tedious process of regaining her abilities. It was discouraging and draining at times, but I kept reminding myself that God was in charge and that His promises were real. That thought was empowering.

I put my arm around Lexi's waist and helped her out of bed. Then, reaching for her hand and clutching her firmly to keep her balanced, we walked slowly and steadily a few yards to the gym. Holding her hand was the thing I cherished most since the accident. Even when she was lying in bed, she'd reach over and grab it, giving me a feeling of deep satisfaction. I enjoyed these moments together. She needed me, needed me next to her, needed my love and encouragement. Putting my life on hold for almost a year as it revolved around her needs changed me. I was happier. Since it was only the two of us most of the day, it bonded our relationship. We connected with a special closeness that many mothers yearn for.

> Blessed is the people that know . . . they shall walk, O Lord, in the light of thy countenance.
> —Psalm 89:15

She had speech, occupational, and physical therapy twice a day for half an hour each. After the three consecutive sessions, she would collapse in bed, ask for more meds, and fall asleep. I didn't allow many visitors in her room because I wanted her undisturbed to keep her strength up. However, one of her friends, Jordan, who was like family, came regularly. Most of the time, Lexi was too physically exhausted to visit, but Jordan was content just to be with her in the room.

One late afternoon, Jordan leaned over Lexi's bed and quietly said, "I'm going to the beach tomorrow, so I won't be able to come see you for a week."

Lexi was still not talking much, so we were slightly startled to hear her whisper back, "Take me with you, please." Her eyes filled with disappointment. It made me teary to hear her soft, but poignant, reply—and my heart sorrowed.

Jordan continued, "It will go by fast, like I'd never been gone."

And, truly, it wasn't long before we realized that, for Lexi, going to the beach might be a possibility sooner than we had hoped. She started to gain her strength back during the third week after her accident. And there was a sense of expectation that she would be walking by herself soon. We felt that God had answered our prayers.

It didn't surprise me to see Lexi so determined to learn to walk again. She had always been competitive, especially in sports. Sometimes during her therapy sessions, I would get lost in my memories of her younger days. Her feisty spirit showed especially when she played basketball. It made me smile to remember some of the banter on the court when she played on the boys Junior Jazz team at eleven years old, and I became lost in my thoughts.

"Look at that. There's a girl on their team!" one of the boys on the opposing team sneered.

The boys glanced at each other smirking. Lexi glared at them with fire in her eyes and her lips drawn tight.

"You'll see," one of her teammates replied defiantly.

Lexi wasn't one to venture hesitantly into a game. She schooled them in the first quarter. Her team cheered and lavished Lex with praise as she grinned.

Her opponents' faces were pinched with panic, and they began to blame each other for their lack of scoring.

"You can't guard a girl?" one boy snapped, giving his friend an icy stare. The smugness on their team had vanished.

"How can I lose to a girl?" another boy muttered as he stomped off the court. Lexi's athletic skill and competitive nature were always surprising to people.

I was pulled from my musings when the physical therapist walked in Lexi's room and announced, "Are we ready for this, Lexi? I think today is the day!"

Lexi had surprised everyone at the hospital by her rapid recovery and her stubborn resolve to do things faster than they thought she should. No one could have imagined on that fateful day in February that she would come as far as she had, especially in such a short amount of time.

Walk in the steps of that faith of our father.

—Romans 4:12

"Let's do this!" Lexi exclaimed, her lips pursed together. I helped Lexi up out of bed, and holding her hand, we walked out of her room. Now, with a therapist on either side holding her steady, we eagerly waited for them to allow her to walk on her own.

She continued haltingly down the main hall when one therapist said, "Okay, we are going to let go of you now."

The therapists kept their hands inches from Lexi's torso in case they needed to catch her. Lexi hesitated momentarily, and then she began to walk on her own, cautiously placing her feet one in front of the other with great precision.

My heart jumped as a wave of joy washed through me. I cheered loudly, bursting with pride, "Way to go Lexi! Look at you!" Although Lexi was still frail, it was one of the most poignant moments of her recovery.

When Lexi got to the end of the hall, her voice cracked with emotion, "I did it." Her face glowed with happiness. By then, my eyes were brimming with tears of joy, and my smile stretched wide, basking in the moment. She had never stopped trying, and now she had triumphed! I moved swiftly to her side to embrace her. The warmth of that moment stretched for a long time.

JD said it best when describing Lexi's recovery:

The pain has been almost unbearable at times. She was intubated multiple times, she suffered a broken leg, and the list goes on. Some might ask why God would allow certain people to suffer so much more than others during their life here on earth.

Joseph of Egypt was one who could have asked the same question. Favored by his father, but secretly hated by his brothers, he was sold into Egypt where he became a slave. But instead of dwelling on his misfortune, he went forth until Potiphar made him overseer in his house. He was then cast into prison when Potiphar's wife lied about Joseph's advances toward her. Again instead of turning against the Lord, he turned toward Him. The Lord was with him in prison, and he was able to interpret dreams. At the appropriate time, he was called out to interpret the dream of Pharaoh, and as a result was made second only to Pharaoh in the land. When his brothers came to collect food during the famine, Joseph made himself known to them and said, "Now therefore be not grieved, nor angry with yourselves, that ye sold me hither: for God did send me before you to preserve life" (Genesis 45:5).

At the beginning of Lexi's accident, our family often asked, "Why did this happen to Lexi? She was so good, so young. Why does she have to suffer?" But as time progressed, we realized that God often gives us trials to bless others' lives: for God did send Lexi before others to preserve life. Just as Joseph saved thousands during the time of famine, Lexi has given spiritual hope and guidance to our family and friends and, perhaps, has saved a life, spiritually speaking. Our Savior, Jesus Christ, went through the hardest trial ever known to mankind, but through His sacrifice, we all can be saved. What a wonderful thing to know that even trials can be a gift from our Heavenly Father. May our trials turn us to the Lord so that we may bless the lives of others too.

Lexi learned quickly to never ask, "Why did this happen? Why am I in so much pain? Why do I have to learn to walk again?" She trusted in God's plan for her. She never wallowed in self-pity or bitterness but was filled with determination. When people asked her how she was feeling, there was intensity in her eyes as she would put on her cheery smile and tell them she was doing well. Her words sunk into my thoughts. I knew how agonizing her injuries were, so her answers always surprised me. She didn't want people to worry about her or feel sorry for her. She knew she had been blessed to be alive, and she was grateful for kind friends, brothers, and sisters, who loved and cared about her.

I love Paul because his journey in life was a lot like each of ours is. We all have our bumps and bruises, some more than others, as we are tossed to and fro upon the sea of life. Sometimes, we will feel cast aside or forgotten as "in the furnace of affliction" (Isaiah 48:10). Hardships, imprisonment, beatings, and toiling to the point of exhaustion were the harsh realities of his life. Yet despite Paul's challenges, he says with full faith, "I will put my trust in him." (Hebrews 2:13).

Like Paul, instead of feeling sorry for herself, Lexi would do the things she could. And as Lexi learned to walk again, she continued to walk with God.

Chapter Twenty-Three

THE MIRACLE OF ARRIVING HOME

We must through much tribulation enter into the Kingdom of God.

—Acts 14:22

Lexi's room was on the eighth floor of the hospital. Sitting on the ledge of her window was the best vantage point to see the trains. That was important because Calvin, Lexi's two-year-old nephew, came to visit her every day, and trains were all he talked about. It didn't hurt that the view was spectacular with the snow-capped mountains in the background.

Cassidy, Calvin's mom, lived in Texas but decided to stay for a month to help me out and be there for Lexi. Knowing how hard it was for a two-year-old to go to the hospital every single day and stay in a cramped, sterile room where he was not allowed to do much of anything, I tried to think of ways to make him happy about returning the following day.

One afternoon, I called out to him in an animated voice just as they were leaving the hospital, "Guess what you get to do tomorrow, Calvin?"

He glanced over his shoulder with eager eyes and said, "What?"

"You get to come to the hospital to see Lexi," I said, trying to put as much expression in my voice as I could.

I was fully expecting him to stomp his feet and tell us he didn't want to come back. But much to my surprise and relief, he spun around to his mom and squealed with glee, "Yay! We're going to the hospital tomorrow," his sweet expression matching his heart.

To have them come each day created a good diversion for me. It was also helpful to have someone to voice my concerns to when Lexi was not moving forward like I wanted. Cassidy was someone Lexi had always looked up to, so Cassidy was able to give Lexi a nod of encouragement when she was about to give up. Lexi had been progressing rapidly physically, but she could not swallow without aspirating (inhaling small particles of food or liquid into her lungs), which sentenced her to a longer stint in the hospital.

In the world ye shall have tribulation: but be of good cheer; I have overcome the world.

—John 16:33

Each time I thought she conquered her swallowing, she would take a drink, nearly gag, and start to cough over and over again. Her face would fall, sadness in her eyes, and she would sigh in frustration. I tried not to show my disappointment, knowing how difficult it must be for her to want to leave the hospital and not be able to, but my joy was dashed. She was also anxious to get the feeding tube out and eat real food again, but for the time being, she was only allowed ice chips.

Two weeks after arriving in the rehab center, she was allowed to eat two spoonfuls of applesauce and two spoonfuls of apple juice two times a day. She was actually given other food options, but she would always ask for the same selection. I was pleased at the prospect of her going home soon.

After a few days, she was able to swallow correctly, and the tube was taken out. Relief swept inside me. We both had suppressed the idea that it could happen so soon, and our eyes widened with shock. The best part about passing the swallowing test? She got to come home! We were all elated.

That same afternoon, she ate her first bite of food. "And this," said Lex, scooping up a spoonful of mashed potatoes, "is the greatest day ever."

However, her mouth and head started to pound after eating only a couple bites of food, so she put down her spoon, and her gentle smile disappeared. She slouched back down on her pillow, her head throbbing, and her body weary. It hurt her to swallow or talk, and touching her head caused her to wince and cry out. At the moment, I had no idea that getting her to eat would be one of the hardest challenges when she returned home. She was a shadow of her former self.

But we rejoiced that Lexi was going home and knew it was a direct answer to the many prayers given on her behalf.

There was a surge of excitement in the rehab center the next day as Lexi got ready to go. Her favorite song began playing over the loud speaker, and her nurse wheeled her around the facility to wave goodbye to nurses, therapists, and staff who had lined the hallway to wish her well and give one last hug.

I was overjoyed to take Lexi home, but it was also heartwarming to see those that had become such a big part of our lives. They had cared for my daughter with cheerful hearts during monotonous and sometime dreary days. I hoped that I had conveyed my appreciation to them sufficiently. It had been an epic struggle to get her this far, but she made it.

We lingered at the elevator doors, allowing Lexi time to remember the enormity of what was taking place. As the heavy glass doors slid open, my heart quickened. A rush of fresh air filled our lungs. There was the smell of spring in the air, which brought a feeling of hope and newness of life. The bright sunshine swept over us and through us, reminding us of the Savior, who had brought to us this miracle.

The ride home, however, was anything but kind. Every little bump and jostle of the car caused Lexi to cry out in pain. I drove as slowly as possible, but to Lexi the trip was excruciating. When we pulled up to our house, I had Lexi sit up. She peered out the car window and saw the hundreds of colored ribbons that neighbors and friends had tied to our bushes and trees. They had done this a few days after the accident. It was a welcoming sight that allowed her to see that she was loved and cared about.

I tenderly and carefully helped her out of the car and into the house. She was greeted by Cassidy and the welcome home posters she had made. We relished the moment. It would have been fun to have friends and neighbors greet her, but her frail body wouldn't have been able to handle it. That day would have to wait.

Although Lexi was steadily getting better, it would not be an easy recovery for her to get back the abilities that she had before. But no matter how slow the progress, Lexi kept trying, kept moving forward. Even though she had to drop out of school and could not walk fast, run, or jump, and still had lingering pain, she was holding fast to hope and cherishing every new day she was given.

The day after Lexi returned home, I became her physical, speech, and occupational therapist. I had taken my oldest daughter, Shae, to similar therapists on a weekly basis and had gone with Lexi to all of her sessions, so I felt confident I could do it. I also knew how excruciating it would be for Lexi to travel in a car again, so staying at home was the best option.

Lexi's clothes were still in the boxes that had been retrieved from her dorm. I decided this would be a good way to facilitate greater mobility, so I playfully asked her, "Lex, would you put your clothes away as part of your therapy?"

> Beloved, think it not strange concerning the fiery trial which is to try you, as though some strange thing happened unto you: But rejoice, inasmuch as ye are partakers of Christ's sufferings; that, when his glory shall be revealed, ye may be glad also with exceeding joy.
>
> —1 Peter 4:12–13

"Of course, I don't mind," Lexi said, shrugging her shoulders. She selected a blue and white flowered blouse, lifting it from the box. But this proved to be quite the formidable task for her.

She slunk down and collapsed in a heap on the carpet after putting away only three shirts. "I can't do this," Lexi said with teary eyes.

I crouched down beside her, drawing my knees beneath my

chin, and reached over to rub her arm in sympathy. "Lexi, I've seen you do more than this at the hospital," I said as I tried to prod her on.

But she just sat and moaned, "I'll try tomorrow. Tomorrow I'll be able to." She blew out her breath in frustration and shot me a pleading look.

I hesitated only for a moment. Keeping busy was paramount. "Just put four more items away. You can do hard things," I reminded her. "Don't give up."

Her left eyebrow arched. "Are you sure?" she asked. But my suggestion was enough of an encouragement for her to gingerly sit back up. She reached in the box to retrieve a pair of socks, and then she put them away. It took only a few more minutes before she crumpled on the floor again, her body spent. She grimaced momentarily, as if sudden pain shot through her.

The next morning, I stood in the doorway surveying Lexi's silhouette sleeping soundly in the dim light. I swallowed quickly. I hated to wake her from her slumber, knowing the only relief from her pain was sleep. She savored the time she had to stay in bed. I gently stroked her forehead, knowing how it soothed her agony, and quietly whispered her name. Blinking her eyes open and stretching her arms, she winced in pain.

We talked for ten minutes before I asked, "Are you ready to sit up now?"

"No," she shook her head emphatically, hugging her soft pillow tightly. "Just give me a few more minutes," she pleaded, fear mingling with unforgotten pain.

While waiting for her to sit up, it occurred to me that this would be a good time to work on her speech therapy.

"What's the capital of Utah?" I asked, trying to jog her memory.

Lexi looked up and rolled her eyes. "Salt Lake. Duh."

"Sorry, Lex, but you know I have to ask." I knew she didn't like my endless round of questioning, but her memory had not completely returned yet.

"Okay, fine," I said, "I will make it more difficult. Okay, who was the confederate general in the Civil War?"

There was a long questioning look. "I—um—I know the answer. It's just sometimes my mind just won't tell me." Her eyes filled with frustration.

"It's okay, we'll come back to it later," I replied, squeezing her arm and continued questioning.

After a half hour of interrogating her, I kindly but firmly insisted she sit up. I refused to let her believe that this was insurmountable.

"But it hurts too much," she cried. Her red, tear-rimmed eyes pleaded up at me. "Let me stay here a little longer please?" It took a little more coaxing before Lexi took a deep breath and sighed, "Okay, I can do this."

Little by little, her pain decreased, although it was hard to see any improvement day to day. Both of us had to put our trust in God.

On Mother's Day, when I walked in her room eating a bowl of cereal, Lexi started to cry. I assumed her tears came because of her head wound, but through her whimpering she managed to tell me that she had wanted to fix me breakfast for Mother's Day. She was distraught and would not be consoled until I suggested that she fix me lunch. Once again, I reflected on the fact that even during her difficult days, she was able to look outward to see what she could do to brighten another person's life.

As she improved physically, Lexi was excited to pull her violin out of its case and play again. But her dreams of having a command of the instrument right away were squashed once she started to play. She handed me her violin and crumpled in a heap on the floor.

"I can't play," she moaned. "I don't want to start over. That's why . . ." Her voice faded.

"That's why what?" I asked.

"That's why I didn't want to try." Her eyes peered through her tousled hair that had fallen gently across her face.

"Yes, you can play," I would remind her. "As long as you keep trying, God will help you. You've been promised." I winked, handing the violin back to her.

"Sorry. No, I'm not trying again," she said.

I knew that the next day she would be willing to face the formidable mountain and that soon I would hear the violin throughout the house again. She was not a quitter.

For some reason, it was easier for her to accept her choppy and mistake-ridden pieces on the piano. After practicing just a few short weeks, it happened: I was upstairs when a familiar sound warmed my heart. I could hear a faint melody float into my bedroom. It dawned on me that it was Lexi playing the piano as serenely as she had before the accident.

> I can do all things through Christ which strengtheneth me.
> —Philippians 4:13

I went downstairs carefully to not disturb her, and edged toward the piano. She was pouring her soul into her music as her slender fingers danced across the ivory keys. When she was finished, I clapped wildly and wrapped my arms around her.

"You did it," I said. "It came back. God keeps His promises." A smile broke across her face as she realized what she had accomplished.

The summer flew by despite the long grueling days of therapy. Lexi was excited to return to college and show that she could make it on her own. I wasn't worried about her—well, maybe I had a twinge of concern—but I knew I'd miss her fiercely. I had spent the last six months taking care of her, and now I had to relinquish my role. The long days together made me even more reluctant for her to leave. But she was ready to face whatever the world was to toss her way.

Once she was back on campus, the classwork proved to be much more difficult than Lexi had anticipated. As the semester progressed, she began to wonder if she would pass some of her writing classes. But with some extra tutoring and lots of effort, she made it through.

I was thrilled now that she was back at school, but I worried about how she'd feel about herself now that her once-flawless face was disfigured. It was remarkable that she didn't receive any cuts on her entire body when she was hit, yet her whole face was scarred from her chin to her forehead. When the doctors suggested we go to a plastic surgeon in a year, Lexi scoffed at the idea.

> For the Lord seeth not as man seeth; for man looketh on the outward appearance, but the Lord looketh on the heart.
>
> —1 Samuel 16:7

"If people don't like me with my scars, then I don't want them to be my friends anyway," she said defiantly. I was surprised and delighted by her candid response. She believed it was her spirit and who she had become on the inside that was important.

Before the accident, she seemed oblivious to the fact that she was beautiful. The truth was her striking blue eyes, golden skin, tall and thin frame, glistening long blonde hair, and radiant smile made her gorgeous. Yet she was humble and untouched by this gift. She had always had the natural ability to think of others before herself. In high school, stylish clothes are an important status symbol, yet Lexi was uninterested in buying name-brand clothes. She wore a pair of shoes that were torn and ripped her entire senior year in high school, but she didn't care. Looking back at her nonchalant attitude toward her looks, I shouldn't have been surprised by her stance now. She had always felt at home in her own skin.

Chapter Twenty-Four

THE MIRACLE OF FOLLOWING HIS FOOTSTEPS

Ye shall be witnesses unto me both in Jerusalem, and in all Judæa, and in Samaria, and unto the uttermost part of the earth.

—Acts 1:8

One day, shortly after Lexi's release from the hospital, I walked in the kitchen to see Lexi hunched over and shuffling her feet as she circled around and around our kitchen table.

"What are you doing?" I asked her.

"My friend said I can't be a humanitarian worker unless I can walk eleven hours a day. I'm practicing. I want to go now," she said with determination.

I couldn't believe her single-mindedness; she was impatient with her body's limitations and pushed herself to her limits. She continued to limp along for a few more minutes, and then meandered over to the couch and slithered down into its comfort.

"I'm not really tired," she announced, trying to hide her fatigue. "My head just hurts." She was exhausted and had a faraway look in her eyes.

She had been begging me for days to take her to the doctor for a physical so she could volunteer to give humanitarian aid somewhere around the globe. But she knew that I would not take her looking so feeble. I was extremely proud of her drive and could not help smiling when I thought of what she might look like to an outside observer. I'm sure they would have called her foolish for even thinking of spending a year and a half helping others and teaching of Christ. Yet we both knew that she would go. It would not be long before the promise that all of her abilities would return was fulfilled.

> For thus saith the Lord God: Behold, I, even I, will both search my sheep, and seek them out.
>
> —Ezekiel 34:11

Two months after her accident, Lexi insisted I get an appointment to see her doctor that week. It didn't matter that she had just gotten her neck brace off the week before. She still could not move her head without moving her entire body.

At our appointment, the first thing the doctor had her do was lie down on the examination table and try to lift her head up off the table. She couldn't do it. This doctor had never seen Lexi before, and after reading the report about her accident and seeing how frail she was, he told her she could only do some volunteer work from home and probably not for at least another year.

I told him emphatically that she had been promised that she would make a full recovery. Not knowing if he believed in God or not, my voice rang with confidence when I told him about the miracles that had transpired in the last few months.

He got teary eyed and said with reverence, "Okay, we will make it happen. You come back in a month, and we will see where you are."

In one month's time, Lexi had improved so rapidly that she was able to drive herself to the doctor's office. The change was dramatic.

"You are a miracle," he said; his voice filled with emotion when he saw her. "You were saved for someone. You have full clearance to go anywhere you want to go."

A whisper of a smile crept across Lexi's face. After getting the okay from this doctor, she then went to each one of her former doctors and got full clearance to be go anywhere in the world with no restrictions.

> *How beautiful upon the mountains are the feet of him that bringeth good tidings, that publisheth peace; that bringeth good tidings of good, that publisheth salvation.*
>
> —Isaiah 52:7

A week after Lexi had signed up to serve, she was driving home from work and thought, *Hey, it's Wednesday. I might get a letter today telling me where I'll be going to give aid. It could be here, but I'm guessing it won't since they told me it would take six weeks longer than normal due to my accident. But still . . .*

With a little bit of hope, she opened the mailbox, timidly peering inside. There it was, the envelope! A rush of emotion swept over her, and she ran inside screaming, "It came! It came!"

> *Follow me, and I will make you fishers of men.*
>
> —Matthew 4:19

Gladness welled up inside me seeing the light of happiness that sprang from her eyes. We waited until a time when family and friends were able to arrive and watch her open the letter telling her where she would be going.

Finally, the long-anticipated hour came, and I was still fighting hard to maintain a calm demeanor. As Lexi stood up in front of the large group, a sudden burst of emotion washed over her, and tears filled her eyes as she began to read her letter from the prophet. Her voice was full of fervor as she told the group that she was going to Hong Kong, China.

She held back a grin that was threatening to erupt. The room exploded with cheers and applause. Then, she burst out laughing, "Just kidding! I'm going to Des Moines, Iowa."

There was a deafening silence, confused faces stared up at Lexi before realizing they had been duped. Then the room erupted with laughter.

Joy engulfed her as she squealed, "I get to serve the people right here in the United States!" She didn't care where she served as long as she got to serve.

And to make it even more poignant, this opportunity had come on the six-month anniversary of her accident. We had not anticipated this joyous day to come so soon. My spirit was soaring. She told me later that it was probably the happiest and most exciting day of her life because she would be able to give back to others after having been richly blessed her entire life.

When Jesus "passed through Jericho . . . there was a man named Zacchaeus. . . . And he sought to see Jesus . . . and could not for the press" (Luke 19:1–3). So too, Lexi found the press of her problems could have kept her from seeing the Savior. But she was like Zacchaes, who did not just stand there in the crowd as it surged. He took matters into his own hands so that he could see the Savior, and "he ran before,

> *When thou art converted, strengthen thy brethren.*
>
> —Luke 22:32

and climbed up into a sycamore tree to see him" (Luke 19:4). He knew we were to be "doers of the word, and not hearers only" (James 1:22). It was after he had done his part that the Savior "looked up, and saw him, and said unto him, Zacchaeus, make haste, and come down; for today I must abide at thy house" (Luke 19:5). Obviously, the Savior, who knows all things, could have spied Zacchaeus in the crowd, but, just as the woman with the issue of blood did, he had to show the Lord through his faith or movement that he would do whatever it took to be near to Him.

Lexi had a press of health problems that could have kept her from going on a humanitarian mission. She could barely walk, eating made her throat and head hurt, and there was always that excruciating pounding in her head. Notwithstanding all of that, she kept walking, moving and pressing forward, showing to the Lord that she would climb that sycamore tree. When God saw her devotion, he called up to her, looking at her clear blue eyes and said, "Lexi come down and sup with me." Locking her eyes with the Savior she "made haste, and came down, and received him joyfully" (Luke 19:6). No more would I miss an opportunity to sup with the Savior.

Chapter Twenty-Five

THE MIRACLE THAT GOD KNOWS US BY NAME

And he healed many that were sick of divers diseases, and cast out many devils.

—Mark 1:34

And whithersoever he entered, into villages, or cities, or country, they laid the sick in the streets, and besought him that they might touch if it were but the border of his garment: and as many as touched him were made whole.

—Mark 6:56

It has been remarkable to take this journey to acknowledge the hand of heaven in Lexi's life.

Some people might say that miracles don't happen in our day. But the God we worship is the same God who healed the lame, gave sight to the blind, and restored hearing to the deaf. Should we not expect that God wants to bless us as much as he did those who lived before us? Paul teaches that we should "seek the Lord, if haply [we] might feel after him, and find him, though he be not far from every one of us" (Acts 17:27).

The parting of the Red Sea provided undeniable evidence of God's divine intervention, and the raising of Lazarus reminds us of His power and love. The miraculous healing of Lexi tells us that God's hand is still in our lives, that he is aware of us, and that all blessings come through Him. I could not remain silent when I was eyewitness to a miracle.

Sometimes, when we don't see miracles in our own lives, we question whether God is really there. We might feel forsaken and lose hope if there is silence in the heavens. But we are not alone. God is refining our souls and stretching our faith to see if we will remain obedient "in the time of [our] tribulation"

> *Who is a God like unto thee, that pardoneth iniquity, and passeth by the transgression of the remnant of his heritage? He retaineth not his anger for ever, because he delighteth in mercy.*
>
> —Micah 7:18

(Judges 10:14), and if we will "be ye valiant" (2 Samuel 2:7), for "the Lord shall be unto thee an everlasting light, and thy God thy glory" (Isaiah 60:19). "He hath delivered [us] out of all trouble" (Psalm 54:7). God allows us to struggle on our own at times so that we can become stronger and better than we were. Eventually, after painful and seemingly endless tutoring, He brings light to our difficult days and peace to our troubled souls. We will be okay because God *will* provide a way.

> *For the commandment is a lamp; and law is light . . . to keep thee from the evil.*
>
> —Proverbs 6:23–24

The Lord didn't put any of us on Earth to be free of

trials, because it's only through adversity that we can become humble and teachable. Our hearts more readily turn to the Lord, knowing that He is the only one that can understand our pain and heartache. He has suffered for us so He can succor us through our personal trials. We cannot do it alone. We must learn to rely on Him and use these trials to change our natures.

When adversity comes, we cannot afford to turn away from God. God knows what is needed for our growth in order for us to become like Him. We need to trust in His plan for us, and listen to the Spirit even when our prayers aren't answered as we would like or in the time frame we would want. We must learn to live the words, "Trust in the Lord with all thine heart; and lean not unto thine own understanding. In all thy ways acknowledge him, and he shall direct thy paths" (Proverbs 3:5–6).

Do we have confidence that the Lord will deliver us in our darkest nights? Do we believe "He shall feed his flock like a shepherd: he shall gather the lambs with his arm, and carry them in his bosom, and shall gently lead [them]"? (Isaiah 40:11). Will we stand with Shadrach, Meshach, and Abed-nego and say, "I know our God will deliver us, *but if not*, I will continue to look upward and trust that He will open a way even when there doesn't appear to be one"?

We are the Lord's sheep, and "he calleth his own sheep by name, and leadeth them out" (John 10:3). He not only hears our prayers, but also leads us out of our troubles. He will answer us because He has told us that He will. But we need to have the courage to wait for His timing. Then, someday, when we kneel at the Savior's feet, we will

> And all flesh shall know that I the Lord am thy Savior.
>
> —Isaiah 49:26

hear His words, "Well done, thou good and faithful servant" (Matthew 25:21).

I know that this one percent miracle was not a once-in-a-lifetime event. I believe the Lord sends small miracles to us daily. Look for them each day and write them down so that you can always remember that God is still a God of miracles.

Conclusion

THE MIRACLE OF ALWAYS REMEMBERING

When your children shall ask their fathers in time to come, saying, What mean these stones? Then ye shall let your children know, saying, Israel came over this Jordan on dry land. For the Lord your God dried up the waters of Jordan from before you, until ye were passed over . . . That all the people of the earth might know the hand of the Lord, that it is mighty.

—Joshua 4:21–24

We read in the scriptures how Christ performed miracles daily among the people. And like those who were witnesses, some of you may have had your hearts "burn within [you]" (Luke 24:32) as you've read through these pages. That feeling is the power of the Holy Ghost testifying to you that Lexi's healing was a miracle in our day and that God is still a God of miracles.

Satan doesn't want us to remember. He doesn't want us in a higher place of peace and unspeakable joy. He doesn't want us to have an unshakable faith in God and His plan for us. We read in the New Testament and in other scriptures of miracles wrought, and yet we find that in just a few short years, those same people forgot the miracles and hardened their hearts.

For example, we read that "the devil, as a roaring lion, walketh about, seeking whom he may devour" (1 Peter 5:8), and that the "god of this world hath blinded the minds of them which believe not, lest the light of the glorious gospel of Christ . . . should shine unto them" (2 Corinthians 4:4). And as a result, they began to disbelieve the wonders and miracles they had seen.

So let us "take heed to thyself, and keep thy soul diligently, lest thou forget the things which thine eyes have seen, and lest they depart from thy heart . . . but teach them thy sons, and thy sons' sons" (Deuteronomy 4:9) and walk with Him through sunshine and storms.

When Christ asked the apostles who the people thought He was, they answered, "John the Baptist: some, Elias; and others, Jeremias, or one of the prophets. He saith unto them, But whom say ye that I am? And Simon Peter answered and said, Thou art the Christ, the Son of the Living God" (Matthew 16:14–16). Yet the night of the Savior's crucifixion, Peter denied the Savior three times. It wasn't until after the Savior was resurrected that Peter's testimony became unshakable. Through Lexi's miracle, I can understand in a small way the change that came over Peter. I thought I knew God before, but I truly know him now. I have searched the scriptures and have received revelations, and "cannot but speak the things which [I] have seen and heard" (Acts 4:20). And having all these witnesses, I have obtained a hope, and faith, which has become "steadfast, unmoveable, always abounding" (1 Corinthians 15:58).

Why did this miracle occur? Why are miracles recorded in

the scriptures? John tells us why: "But these are written, that ye might believe that Jesus is the Christ, the Son of God; and that believing ye might have life through his name" (John 20:31).

I know that it was God that gave our family this one percent miracle. He is involved in every detail of our lives. I have learned that even against all odds that God can bless us with miracles if we don't give up, but turn to him the source of all light and goodness. It is Gods greatest desire to bless us. His love is eternal. We cannot be the same again. We must not be the same again.

Lexi's Afterword

LIFE IN A DIFFERENT PERSPECTIVE

Throughout my life, I was taught that hardships and trials happen to help us learn and become better individuals. I found that having this knowledge ingrained in my heart at a young age helped immensely when I was facing the crisis of my life. I learned to be patient and trust that the tragedy happened for a reason and could be overcome. Though the road to becoming whole again was long, and was harder than the strength that I possessed, I knew it was possible if I turned Heavenward.

Faith in God is what got me through the painful rehabilitation process. Faith is a hope and belief in something that you cannot see or even prove with empirical evidence. I knew God was there and I had a deep understanding that he was kind and merciful. Knowing and trusting in His care helped me to press on and not fall into despair during my most trying moments. In fact, I wanted to follow the example of Job in the Bible, who had everything taken from him, yet he never lost faith in God.

I don't have a recollection of the first three weeks after I was hit by a car. But after that, the experiences I had were forever seared in my memory. The arduous task to relearn the most basic functions of life was not erased from my mind. I was and will be eternally grateful for a mother who faithfully and tirelessly stayed by my side and hold me in her arms. Oh the comfort and the refuge I felt as I lay cradled in her embrace. Her influence and love coupled with my dad's concern motivated me. I also felt the force of angels surrounding me and at times it even felt as if God's arms were lovingly around me as well. I came to see why I needed a Savior—for He shrank far beneath my lowest of lows and gave me the fervor to reach higher. Christ suffered not only for my sins but also for my pains and sicknesses. I needed His power, and I found it when I was submissive and humble before Him.

Yes, God gave me strength through His son Jesus Christ, but I still needed to be motivated and press on in determination. I knew that as the Apostle James stated, "Faith, if it hath not works, is dead, being alone" (James 2:17). I had to act. While I was learning to walk again, the therapists had me climb a flight of stairs. I hated it. It was tedious and agonizing primarily because of the rod in my leg and the fact that the coma had left me with little strength. But I could not be lazy and say, "Oh it's alright, I did a little bit and others will take care of me." I knew that to reach my dreams I had to keep pushing myself, even when the pain was unbearable.

Each time I approached a step and gazed at the seemingly endless flight of stairs, I cringed thinking what an awful journey this was going to be. With each stride, I lifted one foot barely high enough to get onto the next step. On several occasions I scuffed the bottom of my shoe because I wasn't able to lift my leg high enough. The therapists patiently waited with their arms always on my waist, in case I should lose my footing. However, this irritated me, as I desired to do this on my own. I thought, *I am strong and I am able. They must know this by now. I won't fall.* Embarrassed by their constant attention, and frustrated at the little progress I was making, I somehow manage to push on.

A few times they led me outside, and it was glorious! Finally, a change of scenery from the innumerable corridors of white walls. The fresh air in my lungs and the sun on my shoulders was rejuvenating. Oh how I missed the outdoors! In my rejoicing, the therapists directed me around the beautiful flowerbeds. Soon they motioned for me to follow them back inside. *Really?* I mused, *Why? I barely made it out here and you are making me go back inside already? This is uncalled for. I am staying outside.* So, I sat down and wouldn't move. It was unfair that I could only spend a couple minutes outside. I wanted to hold onto it for as long as I could. Nonetheless, it wasn't long before I was exhausted and needed to lie down in bed. Going outside gave me the drive to try harder and stretch myself a little more. A few moments each day in the fresh air became my reward for working hard. I saw the light at the end of the tunnel and I wanted it. I knew I could get it.

Every other day I was required to take a shower, which really doesn't seem difficult, but for me it was a horrible ordeal. The worst part about it was when they brushed my hair after I showered. Oh how it hurt! I let out a scream as each stroke inflamed my tender scalp. They were too rough with the brush. I couldn't take it anymore and groaned, "I hate what they are making me go through. Do they not understand the pain I am in? Why can't they be a little bit easier on me?" I would mumble and moan under my breath while fighting to remain calm and press on.

My mother often told me that all my abilities would come back as it was a promise from God. It calmed my anxious heart to hear her words, but I still wondered if my skills, attributes, and health would actually come back. Would I ever be myself? I didn't like feeling stupid when I would forget words or when I was too feeble to even throw a ball. On top of everything, I even had to relearn how to swallow. It seemed impossible to figure out which tube I should use to get my food down. How in the world could I know the difference between the two tubes in my throat? I was frustrated when over and over again the applesauce would slide down the wrong tube and I had to continue to use the feeding tube.

One day the therapist took me into an x-ray room and gave me a spoonful of applesauce. I closed my eyes and said a quick prayer as I put the food on my tongue. I thought, *Get it down the right tube. Which tube? I have no idea. But let's leave it to luck right now so I can go home.* I don't know how it happened, but the food went down the right tube.

As I entered my home, a feeling of awe and gratitude filled my soul. I knew this moment happened because of the many people that prayed and fasted for me. How could I ever repay them? Tears welled up in my eyes as I thought of people I didn't even know who sacrificed their time to pray for me. In that moment I realized the goodness inside every human being.

At home, I still wrestled with having enough energy to walk, talk, and swallow. Some days all I wanted to do was sleep. The pain in my head, neck, chest, and leg was debilitating and persisted all day, every day. It was hard to see progress from day to day, and it was easy for me to despair, wondering whether I would ever regain my abilities. In quiet moments, I thought of my future and what it would be like. How could I get better? Was it possible? Who was I? What was I going to do with my life? Could I ever return to who I used to be? These questions plagued my mind. During those dark moments, I would be reminded by my mom to trust that God was molding me into who He would have me be. I needed to trust that He loved me and that even if my body wasn't exactly the same, my life could still be joyful because of Him. These thoughts brought me peace and helped me to carry on.

Since the pain was so severe at times, I was desperate to find joy. I treasured having people visit me to bring a diversion. One of my most favorite visitors was my sister Cassidy. She came daily and would always ask, "Do you want me to read to you?" I would look at her with excitement in my eyes and an appreciation for her willingness to spend time with me. After reading a couple chapters from her favorite book, she would close it. I would plead for her to keep going. I looked forward to her coming and would ask my mom regularly, "When is Cassidy coming over? Is she going to bring the book again?" I was grateful for these moments that brought respite as I concentrated on the characters in the story. I came to love my sister even more as I cherished the times she spent with me.

On April Fool's day, Cassidy conjured up an idea to fool our siblings. She carefully took off my neck brace while my mom reminded me several hundred times not to move even one inch while the neck brace was off. Cass put on my neck brace and went outside and started jumping on our trampoline. My mom followed her outside and filmed Cassidy jumping up and down while saying, "Lexi, get off the tramp right now. What are you doing?" Afterward, my mom sent the video to the family. My siblings replied how insane and irresponsible I was to jump on the tramp with a broken neck. My mom, Cassidy, and I laughed in complete victory.

Mingled with the fun and humor were difficult days. Whenever I looked in the mirror, I would see my scars. It didn't bother me a lot, but occasionally I would see pictures of myself before my accident and think, *I was beautiful back then. I used to look pretty.* These thoughts were confirmed as people often expressed amazement when they saw what I used to look like, "That's you?" It hurt, but I had to accept it and get used to people's response to my appearance. The doctor told my parents that I should see a plastic surgeon. The surgeon injected steroids into my scars under my nose and chin. The pain was excruciating, and I dreaded going back to repeat the procedure. I could cope better when my mom gripped my hand as tightly as she could and I would hold my breath as the surgeon drove the needle into my scars, tears streaming down my face. After each visit, I plead with my mom that this would be our last visit. I hated it. Had I not gone through enough pain already? Why did I have to go through more? I didn't care how I looked. Looking back, however I am grateful that my parents insisted that I go because my scars aren't as prominent as they once were.

"Ask, and it shall be given you; seek, and ye shall find; knock, and it shall be opened unto you" (Matthew 7:7). This scripture was a promise I relied on as I returned to college that fall. I was scared to leave home but determined. I experienced both joy and sorrow. It was harder than I thought to comprehend what my professors taught and to understand my assigned reading. I felt lost. I was embarrassed to ask for help thinking I could just do it on my own. I finally relented and sought assistance. But my greatest help again came through God. As I continued to rely on Him, I began to comprehend the concepts taught in my classes.

Each of us can feel lost, scared, or overwhelmed. We might feel our world has flipped upside down. In those moments, we must never forget that we are children of God. He is there. He loves each of us and will never leave us alone. We can come to know Him by reading His word for "we know that all things work together for good to them that love God" (Romans 8:28).

Life has moved on but I will always be mindful of the miracle and the lessons I learned. There are still times where I struggle, where I feel alone or embarrassed by my inabilities or inadequacies. However, I have learned to look for the hand of God in my life and remember the grace He has shown me, whether it be manifest through His word or the works of my family and friends. This perspective I will keep and carry on for the rest of my life. "The Lord [my] God turned the curse into a blessing unto [me], because the Lord [my] God loved [me]" (Deuteronomy 23:5).

I, Alexis Hansen, was born on August 30, 1995, to wonderful parents. I truly have been given a magnificent family, each individual playing their own unique role in my life. My adventuring days are not completely gone (although my daring side has been tamed) but my broken body is now healed. I will forever be reminded of that broken longboard and how God through His power, mercy, and grace, blessed me with a one percent miracle.

QUESTIONS FOR PERSONAL REFLECTION AND DISCUSSION

1. **What have you learned through God's miraculous preservation of Lexi's life?** Has God sent any personal messages to you? What is it that He is trying to teach you?

2. **What is the purpose of trials?** How are they a part of God's love and mercy? What is it about trials that help us grow? What can we do to allow our trials to draw us closer to God instead of pushing us further away from Him? What trials in your life have drawn you closer to God?

3. **What is the purpose of a miracle?** Why did this miracle occur in Lexi's life? What are the other miracles that occurred as a result of Lexi's accident? Is a change of heart a greater miracle than that of physical healing?

4. **How has reading this book changed the way you view prayer?** How have you become more assertive in your prayers? Why is there so much power in gratitude prayers? Why were so many people involved in praying for Lexi?

5. **How can you apply the principles in this book to your life?** What concepts or principles from the book will be most memorable to you? What changes have you made or goals have you set for yourself as a result of what you have read and felt?

ABOUT THE AUTHORS

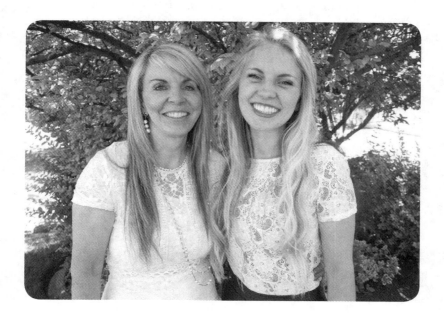

Lexi Hansen is currently a student at Brigham Young University majoring in advertising. In 2015–16, she lived in Iowa teaching the people there about Christ and doing humanitarian work. In high school, she was one of the top tennis players, winning second place at state in doubles. She plays the violin and piano. She is the eighth of nine children. Lexi is in her element when she is doing activities outdoors in the sun, like longboarding, mountain climbing, and playing tennis.

A native of Orem, Utah, Marcia M. Hansen was blessed to be a stay-at-home mom to nine children and is now a grandmother to sixteen. When she was seven, her family traveled halfway around the world to live in Ethiopia and later in Egypt, opening up a world of adventure to her.

After studying art and music at BYU, she taught piano and continues to pursue watercolor, oil painting, and photography. Always an avid reader, devouring any book she could get her hands on, Marcia felt compelled to write her own book after the miraculous events that transpired in the life of her daughter.

Scan to visit

www.marciamhansen.com